MOMS: Developing A Ministry

Paula Hagen and Patricia Hoyt

Resource Publications, Inc.
San Jose, California

Reprint Department
Resource Publications, Inc.
160 E. Virginia Street, #290
San Jose, CA 95112-5876
1-408-286-8508 (voice)
1-408-287-8748 (fax)
www.rpinet.com

Library of Congress Cataloging in Publication Data
Hagen, Paula, 1937-
    MOMS: developing a ministry / Paula Hagen and Patricia Hoyt.—3rd ed.
      p.   cm.
    Includes bibliographical references.
    ISBN 0-89390-534-8
    1. Mothers—Religious life. 2. Church work with women. I. Hoyt, Patricia.
    II. Title.

    BV4529.H265   20001
    259'.085'2—dc21   00-066514

01 02 03 04 05 | 5 4 3 2 1

Editorial director: Nick Wagner
Cover design: Mike Sagara

The floral design used in this book was taken from *Early American Design Motifs*, by Suzanne E. Chapman, published and copyright © 1974 by Dover Publications, Inc., for the Dover *Pictorial Archive* Series.

The excerpt on page 80 is taken from Angeles Arrien, foreword to *The Art of Ritual*, by Renee Beck and Sydney Barbara Metrick (Berkeley, California: Celestial Arts, 1990) and reprinted with permission.

The "Elizabeth and Mary" logo on page 180 is used with permission of the artist, Sister Elizabeth Ruth Obbard, Carmel of Walsingham, Langam Holt, Norfolk, NR25 7BP, England.

To my friends,
who gave me the courage to be true to myself.
— Paula

To Clare O'Mahony,
whose example taught me the ministry of motherhood.
— Patricia

Contents

Part 4: Development of the Ministry

Appendix A: Job Descriptions

Appendix B: Forms

Acknowledgments

The authors gratefully acknowledge the assistance of the people who gave their energy generously in the development of the Ministry of Mothers Sharing. They include Cathy Eilers, who planted the first seed years ago; Lisa Laliberte, Gina Trail, Sue Kieny, and Pat Brooks, from the Young Family Ministry Task Force at St. Timothy's Church, Mesa, Arizona, who developed the initial four-week program; the participants of the first MOMS group at Christ the King Church, Mesa, Arizona, who shared their experience and hopes with us; Raymond Bucher, OSF, and the staff of the Franciscan Renewal Center, Scottsdale, Arizona, who supported MOMS as an outreach program; Vickie Jennett, Nancy Hardy, Peggy Geraghty, Sue Douglas, John and Kathleen Colligan, and Peggy Kenna Redman, who each offered invaluable comments and insights that contributed to the spirit and development of the ministry. Special thanks to the Benedictine Sisters of St. Paul's Monastery, whose wisdom and vision of community gave us strength for the journey, and to the hundreds of parish leaders whose commitment to lay ministry is an ongoing inspiration to us; to our own spiritual support groups who sustained our commitment to the value of this publication; and lastly, to Jim, Christopher, Melissa, Michael, and Rebecca Hoyt, who tolerated with admirable patience the long hours that we have devoted to this book.

Preface

Why Have a MOMS Group in Our Community?

If you have picked up this book, it may be because you are a curious and creative kind of person looking for something that seems to be missing in today's church community. Maybe you see young families wanting to belong; single parents expressing feelings of alienation; two-career parents struggling to live Christian values in the marketplace. Maybe you hear people express a feeling of powerlessness in their neighborhoods, alienation in a bustling, corporate world of confusing values. They ask: "Where do I fit?" If so, you are one of thousands of concerned, active Christians who are in search of the missing ingredient in our communities today.

America's churches have never been as varied as they are today. Some churches are closing, others are forming, some are struggling for spiritual renewal, and still others are full of new life and vigor. Leaders frequently find that although their church is a hive of activity, something is missing. Professional ministers offer an array of excellent programs to lift the community out of lethargy; however, they see no deep-seated spirit of renewal.

Ministry of Mothers Sharing (MOMS) is one innovative way to make a change in this pattern. This gentle program of self-awareness and awakening to the spirituality of motherhood has been tremendously successful in bringing about a sense of belonging, hospitality, faith sharing, and genuine community.

The advantage of MOMS is that it serves two purposes. On the one hand, it is an eight-week experience for mothers to come together, share their stories, and bond by gaining insight into their current mission in the world. On the other hand, it provides an important element missing from many of today's churches: that of hospitality. The art of hospitality is more than being greeted with a smile on Sunday outside church. It is providing a safe place for persons to gather, to tell their story, to be unconditionally accepted. From this kind of genuine hospitality, people begin to experience themselves as Church.

Origins and Development of MOMS

The Ministry of Mothers Sharing was born out of a Young Family Ministry Committee in Mesa, Arizona. A group of parents with young children indicated that, as a follow-up to the baptism of their infants, they would like resources or ideas for beginning family rituals in their homes. They were searching for ways to strengthen their sense of family and their feeling of belonging to the community. They were enthusiastic about learning with other parents and were motivated by a desire to express their faith with their young children.

So, Mothers of Young Children Spiritual Support Group was born. A support-group model was chosen because participants wanted to get to know each other in a safe environment. Practical topics like self-esteem, stress, feelings, values, and the importance of networking with other Christian families made the first series a huge success. The group continued beyond the initial six weeks to talk about even more practical personal issues such as medical problems, childcare, financial problems, family of origin issues, couple communication, parenting skills, dealing with anger, and so on. The women were so motivated that they were willing to learn the communication skills necessary for the group to continue. They began to experience the process of adults learning from each other and recognized this as peer ministry.

Within a year, there were sixty people involved in the Childcare Ministry, Family Ministry, Liturgical Ministry, and other areas in the church community. Several others were interested in creating a Facilitator Training program so that they could continue to organize themselves and develop their skills as facilitators of small groups.

Since that time, the name has changed to Ministry of Mothers Sharing (MOMS), and the ministry has spread and continues to grow nationwide.

This book is a response to the hundreds of people who have asked for help in starting MOMS in their area. We have attempted to provide a practical guide to establishing an initial eight-week program. We have included job descriptions and guidelines which empower participants to discover their own resources and to pass on the experience to other women in the community. We hope that after examining this book, the community leader can confidently mobilize a team of people and create a ministry that will meet the needs of his or her own community.

Introduction

What Is MOMS?

The purpose of MOMS is to create in women an awareness of the inner sacred self, while at the same time teaching them new ways to inspire, encourage, and affirm each other. Through the process of personal and spiritual growth, women have the opportunity to clarify their values, claim their own giftedness, and bring these new strengths to their family relationships and to the Christian community.

What Does a MOMS Program Look Like?

MOMS is an eight-week journey that leads a group of women through an experience of peer ministry, self-discovery, mutual support, and prayer. Participants use the companion volume, *MOMS: A Personal Journal* by Paula Hagen with Vickie LoPiccolo Jennett. Each two-hour session deals with issues that are common concerns in today's world. In sequential order, the participants explore:

- **Session 1: Self-Esteem and Self-Acceptance**
  What choices influence my self-esteem?
  Where am I with my self-acceptance?

- **Session 2: Stress, Worries, and Anxiety**
  What can I do to recognize and deal with stress productively?

- **Session 3: Everyday Spirituality**
  What is my image and experience of spirituality and ministry?

- **Session 4: Feelings**
  How can I name, claim and accept my own feelings and deal with them in my own way?

- **Session 5: Personal Growth**
  How am I being challenged to grow at this time in my life?

- **Session 6: Expressing Values in Friendships**
  What values do I express in my relationships?

- **Session 7: Celebration of New Beginnings**
  Do I feel I belong to this Christian community? How do I celebrate that belonging?
- **Session 8: Discernment: Continuing the Journey**
  What choice do I want to make for my continued personal and spiritual growth? Each participant shares her decision about her choices.

What Do I Need to Start a MOMS?

MOMS is essentially peer ministry. To ensure proper development of MOMS, a Staff Liaison who is committed to lay ministry is critical. This staff person may be hired and paid a stipend to pilot this ministry, or may be an existing staff member who takes on the extra duties of this ministry. He or she will find it helpful to read *Called and Gifted for the Third Millennium: Reflections by U.S. Bishops on the 30th Anniversary of the Decree on the Apostolate of the Laity from Vatican II Council.* The principles therein are those which underlie MOMS.

The church must make a commitment to the training of a core team of lay ministers. This core team will, in time, become the energy that leads the MOMS and maintains the bond to the community. Initially, however, unless your church has already developed a solid lay ministry, the Staff Liaison will direct, energize, and give confidence to the newly-formed team.

The structure proposed in this book for the setting up of MOMS will require adaptation to fit the structure of your own community. The important thing is to lay a good foundation that will make MOMS an integral part of your community—not a separate entity. The Staff Liaison is in the key position to integrate these women and families into the larger local Christian community.

What Does It Cost?

Financial restrictions are a concern of church leaders already on a tight budget. Specific expenses of MOMS are outlined in the section Getting Started, which includes a sample startup budget.

Research indicates that people value and participate more fully in experiences for which they pay. The community or sponsor establishes a fee and provides scholarships for those in need. The suggested fee ranges from $20-$50, depending on the socio-economic status of the participants and the church's ability to subsidize.

MOMS is often sponsored by Family Ministry and subsidized by an existing women's organization that wants to attract new members or provide a family service. Adult Education departments have funded an eight-week pilot experience, seeing MOMS as an entry-level adult education offering.

What's Happened in Other Communities?

Church communities where MOMS is active consistently notice the emergence of a new, dynamic energy as a result of this ministry. Below are the comments of various ministry leaders regarding the impact of MOMS:

"During the phase of life when making the care of children a primary commitment, mothers often feel the despair of being trapped by the solitude of their role. Many women often lack the time to develop intimate, supportive friendships that are so necessary for the development of positive self-esteem. The MOMS program is a personal call to friendship for these women. These groups have done more than provide a support system for the women involved. For most participants, it has been the gateway into church ministry."

"Two MOMS groups recently asked for help in moving to a deeper level of spiritual awakening and to a better understanding of their faith. When the Office of Christian Formation received the request for help from the groups, there was much rejoicing. The desire for adult education was emerging from the people! The participants of those MOMS groups joined a parish course on Women's Spirituality later that year."

"MOMS has fulfilled many needs of new and young families in an older, well-established parish. Women and their families who wanted to become more involved in the life of the community but had not known a way to "break in" connected with leaders that were already participating in ministry. This networking provided the avenue for them to become involved. The MOMS has served as a way of uniting mothers and has allowed a new awakening within our church. Sprinkled throughout every parish function, there are MOMS graduates, and a new spirit of comradery abounds. New and lasting friends are made in each group, further connecting the church members. MOMS sponsors evenings of renewal and mini-retreats for the entire congregation."

"Until recently, families with young children suffered from a sense of isolation. They felt as if they did not belong to the community. In the fall of 1988, the Director of Adult Education introduced the Ministry of Mothers Sharing to the community at St. Thomas. The acronym MOMS was coined by one of St. Thomas' more ambitious participants."

Part 1

Getting Started

Quick-Start Method

Some people (staff or volunteer) have skills in facilitation and program development and may be able to start a MOMS group without spending a lot of time and effort setting up a Core Team or training facilitators. The checklist below will help such people begin immediately.

Checklist for a Quick Start

☐ Read the Job Description for Staff Liaison.

☐ Select a quiet place and convenient time to meet.

☐ Arrange to offset costs by subsidizing from an education budget.

☐ Order 6-8 copies of *MOMS: A Personal Journal* and 3 copies of *MOMS: Facilitator's Guide.*

☐ Personally invite ten to twelve mothers to participate, or use MOMS with an existing mothers' group as a pilot program.

☐ Mail the "Letter of Welcome" and "What to Expect in Ministry of Mothers Sharing" list to each participant. See Appendix B for samples.

☐ Prepare yourself by using the Session Outlines and Prayer Rituals in this book.

☐ Recruit a Core Team from the participants to develop the ministry.

If you choose to use the Quick Start method, turn to the section for Session Outlines and consult the section on Prayer Rituals.

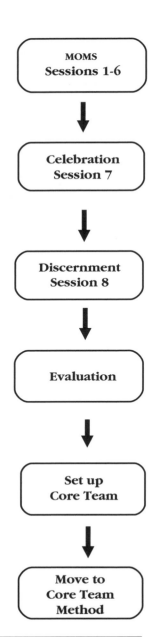

MOMS
Sessions 1-6

↓

Celebration
Session 7

↓

Discernment
Session 8

↓

Evaluation

↓

Set up
Core Team

↓

Move to
Core Team
Method

Core Team Method

This method emphasizes developing a Core Team. The Staff Liaison is committed to using job descriptions to recruit and empower a Team who will provide the foundation for long-term development of the ministry.

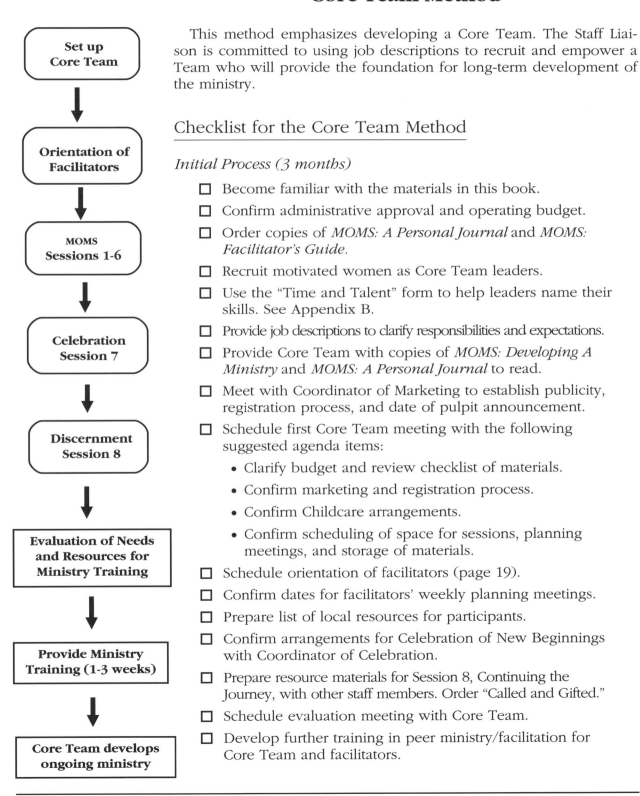

Set up Core Team

↓

Orientation of Facilitators

↓

MOMS Sessions 1-6

↓

Celebration Session 7

↓

Discernment Session 8

↓

Evaluation of Needs and Resources for Ministry Training

↓

Provide Ministry Training (1-3 weeks)

↓

Core Team develops ongoing ministry

Checklist for the Core Team Method

Initial Process (3 months)

☐ Become familiar with the materials in this book.

☐ Confirm administrative approval and operating budget.

☐ Order copies of *MOMS: A Personal Journal* and *MOMS: Facilitator's Guide.*

☐ Recruit motivated women as Core Team leaders.

☐ Use the "Time and Talent" form to help leaders name their skills. See Appendix B.

☐ Provide job descriptions to clarify responsibilities and expectations.

☐ Provide Core Team with copies of *MOMS: Developing A Ministry* and *MOMS: A Personal Journal* to read.

☐ Meet with Coordinator of Marketing to establish publicity, registration process, and date of pulpit announcement.

☐ Schedule first Core Team meeting with the following suggested agenda items:

- Clarify budget and review checklist of materials.
- Confirm marketing and registration process.
- Confirm Childcare arrangements.
- Confirm scheduling of space for sessions, planning meetings, and storage of materials.

☐ Schedule orientation of facilitators (page 19).

☐ Confirm dates for facilitators' weekly planning meetings.

☐ Prepare list of local resources for participants.

☐ Confirm arrangements for Celebration of New Beginnings with Coordinator of Celebration.

☐ Prepare resource materials for Session 8, Continuing the Journey, with other staff members. Order "Called and Gifted."

☐ Schedule evaluation meeting with Core Team.

☐ Develop further training in peer ministry/facilitation for Core Team and facilitators.

Continuing Process (Long-Term Development)

- ☐ Schedule monthly Core Team meetings to be conducted by Coordinator of MOMS. Staff Liaison need not attend.
- ☐ Prepare annual budget and review quarterly.
- ☐ Review evaluations quarterly.
- ☐ Supervise ongoing development of Core Team.
- ☐ Arrange for continued facilitator and lay ministry training opportunities.

Regardless of the method chosen, the Staff Liaison is the primary link between the MOMS Core Team and the pastoral staff of the community. The chart below shows the relationship between all members of the Core Team.

Organization Chart for a MOMS within a Christian Community

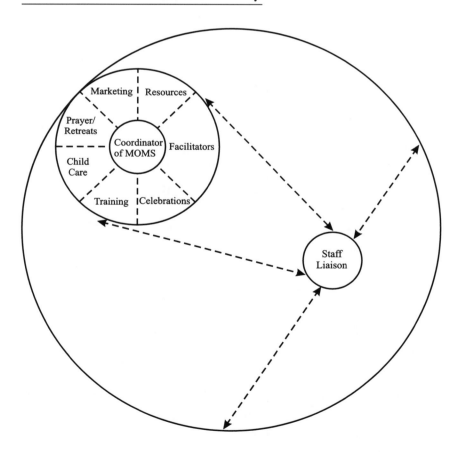

Summary of Position Descriptions

Full job descriptions are contained in Appendix A. Some smaller congregations may be able to function with a smaller Core Team, wherein each person fulfills more than one role.

Staff Liaison

The Staff Liaison is a member of the pastoral staff of the community—for example, a deacon, director of Pastoral Care, director of Christian Formation or Family Ministry—who takes on the responsibility for initiating and developing the MOMS within the community.

Core Team

The MOMS Core Team is composed of a group of leaders who accept a leadership role with the Staff Liaison. Together they make decisions and recommendations in these areas:

- annual calendar of events
- marketing
- MOMS sessions
- leadership training in peer ministry
- budget
- annual goal setting and evaluations

This process of working together on these tasks empowers the leaders to grow in their own spirituality as well as in their call to ministry.

Each member makes at least a six-month to one-year commitment to attend monthly meetings for mutual spiritual support and decision-making with the Team. Some training in peer ministry is highly recommended.

Coordinator of MOMS

This person assists the staff in developing a team of lay ministers. She establishes a communication schedule, an evaluation process, and ongoing training and affirmation for lay leaders.

Coordinator of Marketing

This person represents the church community and MOMS to potential participants. Through appropriate use of a variety of media, she raises awareness among the larger community of the benefits of MOMS and peer ministry.

Coordinator of Facilitators

This person is a skilled facilitator who helps to develop these skills in teams of facilitators. The team consists of the Prayer Leader, the Guardian Angel, and the Presenter. (Specific job descriptions for team members are provided in Appendix A.)

Coordinator of Childcare

If childcare is offered during MOMS, quality childcare is a must. The Coordinator of Childcare has the responsibility of establishing this aspect of the ministry.

Coordinator of Prayer Ministry/Retreats

This person develops a prayer community of persons who are praying for the spiritual needs of each participant. Mornings of prayer, evening reflection, or day-long retreats may become part of her ministry.

Coordinator of Resources

This person brings together the concerns and talents of all the women, especially those of new participants. She organizes and manages parish and community resources for the continued development of ongoing groups and the ministry.

Coordinator of Peer Ministry Training

This person is responsible for coordinating the tasks needed to ensure quality peer ministry training, evaluation, and support of facilitators.

Coordinator, Celebration of New Beginnings

This person is responsible for coordinating the tasks needed to provide the celebration dinner for the seventh session. She supervises a group of peers who plan and provide luncheons for training sessions. She evaluates these events.

Marketing MOMS

Marketing MOMS takes a good salesperson. It means explaining the program in an accurate, enthusiastic way that will attract the target audience: mothers in the church community. Publicity is just part of the marketing process. This phase of marketing requires gathering accurate information and making sure it reaches those you want to attract. Attraction is an equally important element in marketing. Prospective participants will need to know why they should attend this program, what benefits it will bring to them.

Publicity Team

The Coordinator of MOMS recruits someone with experience in public relations and writing to lead the team. Advertising in the newsletter or bulletin may attract a skilled writer. This person may volunteer to do the publicity or give advice to the publicity team, who will distribute information to the community.

Accurate Information

Explain MOMS as follows:

Who: Women who are engaged in the spiritual and physical upbringing of their children. Women who may live stressful lives. Women who live with many demands on their time and energy. Women who need a place to receive personal and spiritual nurturing.

What: The Ministry of Mothers Sharing (MOMS) creates in women an awareness of the inner sacred self while at the same time teaching them new ways to inspire, encourage, and affirm each other. Through the process of personal and spiritual growth, women have the opportunity to clarify their values, claim their own giftedness, and bring these strengths to their family relationships and to the Christian community.

When: Include beginning and ending dates as determined by church or community, day of the week, starting and ending times (two-hour sessions).

Where: Give clear address and directions to the building or room.

Cost: To be determined by church or community.

Marketing Techniques

Seasonal marketing is a concentrated, specific effort to draw attention to the MOMS, six weeks prior to the start of a new series. There may also be certain annual community events that offer opportunities to publicize MOMS. However, *word of mouth publicity is the most influential*. The participant who encourages a friend or neighbor to attend is the most effective motivator.

Fliers and Distribution

For an attractive and professional flier, include an explanation of MOMS (as above), a registration form, and phone numbers of one or two MOMS leaders. If childcare is offered, provide a childcare registration on the same form. A sample flier and registration form are in Appendix B.

Distribute fliers regularly to the various ministries or areas in the community. Some examples follow.

Baptism Class

Insert fliers in the baptismal orientation packet so all receive the information. Ask a MOMS leader to make an appearance at each class and briefly describe the benefits of the MOMS.

Church Registration

Insert fliers in the Welcoming Packet given to new members to reach mothers new to your community.

Formational Ministries

Send fliers home with each child attending classes. In September and January, send promotional material for inclusion in the school newsletter. Personally invite new members joining the faith community and welcome them to attend a MOMS session or Celebration of New Beginnings.

Childcare Ministry

Hand out fliers and personally invite women.

Pulpit Announcement

An announcement on Sunday is an effective way to communicate to everyone. Choose a person with public speaking skills so he or she is brief, clear about the facts, and articulate about the concrete benefits of the ministry. MOMS leaders reinforce the pulpit announcement by giving out clear registration forms, fliers, and additional information. See Appendix B for sample.

Posters

Make attractive posters using art that welcomes all kinds and ages of mothers (single, adoptive, employed, etc.).

Place posters on bulletin boards and in entrances where all can see them.

Church Bulletin

Keep announcements short and informative.

Be sensitive to language. "We" and "you" can be alienating words, projecting the image of a club: "We belong and you do not."

Use the active voice rather than the passive voice: "MOMS offers women an opportunity to meet others..." instead of "Mothers will be given the opportunity in MOMS to..."

The Registration Process

The Registration Form

The registration process begins the moment someone has completed and submitted the registration form (see Appendix B) to the publicity team. The team reviews the registration form to see if prospective participants have grasped the purpose of MOMS. Occasionally, someone is looking for a parenting program, a Scripture study, a prayer group, or therapy.

The Phone Call

If there is a doubt about the expectations of a participant, the Coordinator of Marketing makes a clarifying phone call. This is essentially a screening process. The Coordinator helps the person choose a more appropriate program or service if necessary. She keeps a record of the person and the result, in order to invite her to attend MOMS at another time. All information acquired during this process is kept confidential.

The Letter of Welcome

Ten days before the first session begins, a team member prepares and mails a welcoming letter and a copy of the handout "What to Expect in Ministry of Mothers Sharing" (Appendix B) to each of the participants. The checklist below may be helpful to make sure that the letter contains all suggested information:

- ☐ Use the church or community letterhead.
- ☐ Date (ten days before first session).
- ☐ First paragraph: Time and dates of MOMS group.
- ☐ Second paragraph: Check-in time and place.
- ☐ Third paragraph: Childcare information, if offered.
- ☐ Fourth paragraph: Facilitator team.
- ☐ Fifth paragraph: Preparatory reading.
- ☐ Sixth paragraph: Comments defining the ministry.
- ☐ Seventh paragraph: Contact person and phone number.
- ☐ Signed by Staff Liaison and lay leader.
- ☐ Enclose a copy of "What to Expect in Ministry of Mothers Sharing."

You may want to highlight a check-in time for childcare so nobody comes late to the first session.

The Childcare Arrangements

Quality childcare is an essential component of a successful ministry; therefore, the Childcare Coordinator (paid or volunteer) is part of the Core Team. See job description of Childcare Coordinator (Appendix A) and note childcare information on the registration form (Appendix B).

Financial Planning

The sample budget presented here does not reflect the salary or stipend of a Staff Liaison or Childcare Coordinator. Ideally, each community adjusts its personnel budget to compensate the staff for time spent in developing a new ministry. As the ministry grows, many communities allot a budget for facilitator training and lay leadership.

MOMS is designed so that there is a minimal initial cost to the church or community. Start-up costs are recouped in the registration fee or underwritten by a sponsoring women's organization or ministry. Later these fees are used to provide facilitator training and lay ministry training as needed. Financial planning is an essential part of any ministry development.

There are three simple steps to financial planning. The Staff Liaison or Coordinator of MOMS:

1. Prepares a simple budget prior to beginning, based on projected costs and income.
2. Keeps a log of all expenses and income as they occur during the eight-week period of the group.
3. Prepares a report of actual expenses and income after the group's last session is over and makes any needed adjustments in the budget.
4. Prepares the annual budget each year based on the increased cost of books, supplies, and training needed.

The sample budget on the next page is for use as a model.

Financial arrangements for childcare will vary from one community to another, depending on the facilities available. The Coordinator of Childcare develops a financial budget and keeps separate records of income and expenses.

Sample Start-Up Budget

To begin or pilot MOMS, you need to present a "start-up" budget to the Pastor or Staff Liaison. The following budget is for a group of thirteen women: three facilitators and ten participants.

Projected Initial Expenses

Quantity	Item	Price Per Item	Total
10	*MOMS: A Personal Journal*	$ 11.95	$ 119.50
3	*MOMS: Facilitator's Guide*	$ 23.95	$ 71.85
1	*MOMS: Developing a Ministry*	$ 39.95	$ 39.95
13	*Called & Gifted for the Third Millennium*	$ 5.00	$ 65.00
13	Butterfly Magnets	$ 2.00	$ 26.00
13	Votive Candles	$ 2.00	$ 26.00
13	Serenity Cards	$ .50	$ 6.50
1	Large Candle	$ 8.00	$ 8.00
1 each	Prayer table, tablecloth, music cassette tape	$ 30.00	$ 30.00
	Markers, pencils, nametags	$ 20.00	$ 20.00
	Fliers, photocopying, postage, timer	$ 50.00	$ 50.00
	Total Expenses		**$462.80**

Projected Initial Income

10	Registered Participants @ $30.00 each =		$ 300.00
	Total Income		**$ 300.00**
	Projected Initial Cost to the Parish (Income - Expenses)		**<$162.80>**

Most experienced Pastors, Staff Liaisons, and Lay Leaders know that they cannot initiate a ministry that serves the needs of people without adequate funds for training, books, supplies, and staff involvement. All viable ministries have an investment of time and money. Lay leaders—especially the facilitators—invest a great deal of time and energy to minister to their peers. The parish needs to assume the cost of Leaders' books and training to assure qualified trained leadership.

Additional Costs That Need to Be Considered to Develop a Ministry

This budget does not include childcare or cover any expenses for "Session 7: Celebration of New Beginnings." Initially, the Coordinator of the Celebration needs to plan a celebration, obtain a budget for food and beverages, and arrange for a speaker (approved by the Parish Staff Liaison or Pastor) who is paid a stipend to help ensure quality content.

After the initial session, the Coordinator of the Core Team needs to plan and propose a MOMS budget for continued training, resources, speakers at Celebrations, etc., through the Staff Liaison and/or Pastor. Since this is a ministry, it is best to establish with the Pastor the need for a MOMS account for income and expenses. An annual budget needs to be prepared to allow for the increased cost of books, supplies, and training as the ministry develops and includes more people.

Continued Development

The following costs depend on the resources available in the local community:

- Lay ministry training (i.e., communication skills, stages of group development, theology of lay ministry, models of peer ministry)
- Facilitator training (i.e., assertiveness skills, active listening, theology of grace, empowerment, models of adult education)
- File and storage space for materials
- Good tape recorder and meditation tapes

Agenda: Facilitator Team Orientation

The Staff Liaison and the Coordinator of Facilitators usually conduct this meeting. After the initial pilot session, the Coordinator of Facilitators conducts the meeting. Record questions and concerns for the end of the meeting.

1. Prayer led by Prayer Leader. Use the Opening Prayer in *MOMS: Facilitator's Guide*, Session 1.

2. Confirm each team member's job description (Prayer Leader, Guardian Angel, Presenter). You can make changes within your team.

3. Review importance of planning meeting. See page 29.

4. Review checklist for Session 1 in *MOMS: Facilitator's Guide*.

5. Read "Key Concepts for Facilitators on the Team." See page 20.

6. Refer to "Tips for Facilitators," page 24.

7. Review "What to Expect" (Appendix B).

8. Emphasize the importance of the Assessment Tool for Referral Form (see page 161) and the Certificate of Achievement Preparation Form (see page 159).

9. Set date and time for seven team planning meetings (Sessions 1–6 and Session 8).

10. Set date for facilitator evaluation meeting with Coordinator of MOMS and/or Staff Liaison. See Facilitator Evaluation Form, Appendix B.

11. Note questions and concerns for Core Team or Staff Liaison.

12. Closing Prayer: What are your greatest hopes and fears for yourself in this ministry?

Materials Needed for Facilitator Orientation

- highlighters and prayer candle
- list of participants' names and phone numbers for attendance sheet and certificate form
- orientation materials for facilitators: Job Descriptions (Appendix A), Assessment Tool for Referral, Certificate of Achievement Preparation Form, What to Expect (Appendix B)
- copies of *MOMS: Facilitator's Guide, Called and Gifted* with Study Guide, and Vatican Council II Fact Sheet
- list of local resources to be handed out at Session 4

Facilitator Team Orientation

The Staff Liaison is the person who organizes a schedule of meetings, to include an initial orientation meeting with the three-member Facilitator Team.

At that first meeting, the Staff Liaison clarifies job descriptions and addresses questions or concerns. The meeting needs to be clearly structured and positive to model for the Facilitator Team how subsequent planning meetings should take place. (The Staff Liaison's presence at later planning meetings may not be necessary if the presenter is confident enough to conduct the planning process.)

Key Concepts for the Facilitators on the Team

There are fourteen concepts that need to be clearly articulated and discussed at the orientation meeting if the facilitators are to properly understand the purpose of—and their role in—the MOMS. The Staff Liaison explains the concepts as follows:

MOMS: A Personal Journal

The Journal contains concepts or intellectual ideas. Your role as a facilitator is to give practical examples of how these concepts fit in your life. Emphasize how they do or do not fit for you, not how they should fit in your life or somebody's life. Your honesty and openness will help the participants think about and express their own experience. Having witnessed your example, participants will be stimulated to think about their own experience and be invited to try to share it.

Defining the Role of Facilitator

You are not a teacher who tells the participants what is right or wrong. You are there to create a hospitable and safe place where women can share their thoughts, pray, and get to know other women. You do not have the answer to another woman's concerns; you can only create a space and atmosphere where she can identify her personal concerns and gradually find the answer inside herself.

Peer Ministry

Most of us grew up with a parent-child learning experience of the church. The pastor, minister, or sister was in the parenting or authority role. Ministry of Mothers Sharing is built on a different model, peer ministry: where each person in the group is respected as an equal in her ability to contribute to the success of the group. To achieve this, you as facilitators need to show great respect for the ideas, feelings, and experiences of each participant. Good communication skills and an environment of hospitality and openness are essential for peer ministry to happen.

Confidentiality

Confidentiality is an essential component of a successful group. You cannot build trust without it. At the first session, emphasize its importance with a clear, simple statement such as, "What's said in the group stays in the group." In later sessions, it is a good idea to mention it from time to time. Use a casual tone, so that you do not give the impression of "parenting" the group.

Hospitality

You, as a team, offer participants what is often their first real invitation to be a part of the community. The Guardian Angel's telephone calls—asking how participants are enjoying the experience, encouraging feedback, following up on absences—are vital for the creation of an atmosphere of welcome. Remember that all feedback, including negative comments, must be received with appreciation. Consider criticisms or negative reactions as "recommendations for improvement." The appropriate response will often be: "I appreciate your being honest with me, and the team will certainly keep your feedback in mind as we plan future sessions." In this way, participants will feel truly valued and accepted.

The Family Perspective

The experience these women have over the eight-week period will affect their lives and the lives of their families. It is important to acknowledge that change and to give it a positive direction. The friendship social, scheduled after the second session, offers the chance for a husband or significant friend (male or female) to meet and share with this new circle of friends. A husband may lower his anxiety about "what is happening to his wife" if he begins to feel a part of the experience. The friendship social also allows some women an opportunity for role reversal: often it is they who are invited to attend the husband's social gatherings. A simple prayer ritual to open and close the gathering will add a new dimension to the social occasion.

Bonding

It is crucial to encourage the participants to call each other, go out for coffee, and generally begin to form friendships with each other during these eight weeks. This will give them the opportunity to practice the skills discussed in the MOMS group. Drawing one another's names at the end of each session may encourage the shy person to reach out and call another person.

Commitment

People often feel that their commitment to a group is a personal decision and concerns only them. That is true only during the first session, when participants are often still unsure if the MOMS is for them. After that, the sharing process becomes a group endeavor, and everybody's presence is important. Absenteeism creates insecurity among participants. As facilitators, you will need to encourage participants to make these eight weeks their top priority.

Prayer

Create a prayerful and sacred environment in your gathering room. Pay attention to the choice of attractive material and quality candles for the prayer table. Allow plenty of quiet time for participants to become centered—focused on the prayerful experience. Use the same environment and music each week to provide continuity. The Prayer Sponsors provide a spiritual support for the participants, and their attendance at the Celebration of New Beginnings dinner strengthens the networking and experience of community.

Content

There are whole courses and books on each topic covered in the *Journal*. This experience offers a sampling of topics arranged to build trust in the group. These topics are in the Key Concepts section at the beginning of each session. These will help you stay focused amid the variety of ideas that will emerge. Writing the Key Concepts (word or phrase) on the board may help you keep the group focused on the topic. Try to stay as close to the timeline as you can so participants gain the maximum benefit from the time available. Encourage participants to continue certain discussions after the session.

Facilitator Journaling

Keeping a journal can be one of the most rewarding things you can do for yourself. A journal is a private place where you can record situations, see meanings and patterns in your life, capture unique experiences, and express your feelings. A journal is a tool to help you listen to yourself. It is crucial that you complete your *MOMS: A Personal Journal* and record your observations on your reflection page in the Session Outlines in this book.

Referrals

Some women may get into issues too heavy or problem-oriented for peers to be able to handle. You as a team will need to keep the group focused on the theme. Later, the team and the Staff Liaison may have to skillfully redirect any participants who have issues that require counseling with a professional. Appendix B contains an assessment tool for the team to use in referring somebody to the Staff

Liaison. Be sure to read it to help you identify those who need referral. The Staff Liaison will make available to the participants a list of professional resources within the community. This is all some participants will need for future reference.

Adult Learning Model

Adults have a wealth of experience and knowledge to bring to the learning adventure. Your primary task as a facilitator team is to create an environment of trust in which there can be a non-judgmental sharing of ideas and feelings. Try to keep the sessions positive and lively.

Tears

Occasionally, some women are moved to tears during the MOMS sessions. Tears are natural and normal. It may help to think of them as a prayer from the soul. Accept them with ease. Encourage the participants to be comfortable with their own tears and to accept the tears of others without anxiety. After accepting their tears, help them put words on the feelings. A box of tissues placed in clear sight of the group is practical and may help put participants at ease.

Tips for Facilitators

Facilitators generally find that the hardest part of their job is staying on schedule, staying on the topic, and dealing with difficult situations. Intervening gently to redirect the conversation is a learned skill. The following are some suggestions to help you.

Staying on Schedule and on the Topic

Set clear boundaries and healthy time limitations.

- Be clear about your own goals and agenda. Read aloud the objectives for the session and clarify them for the group.
- Emphasize that all participants will learn most if they continue discussion of the topic and its practical applications between sessions. There is not enough time during the sessions for lengthy discussions.
- Your tone of voice and body language can help keep the discussion moving. Stand up or lean forward as you firmly suggest moving to the next topic.
- Help somebody stay on track by asking, "I am not following you. Is this related to our topic today?"

Dealing with Difficult Situations

Facilitator or Problem-Solver?

When someone asks you to be the problem-solver, counselor, or advice-giver, redirect them in one of these ways:

- "I am not comfortable problem-solving in a group. Let's talk after the session and see if we can come up with some ways for you to address your situation."
- "I don't have the skills to solve that situation. If you like, we can talk after the session about some resources that are available to provide help in that situation." Have available for all participants a list of resources in the local community.
- "You obviously have some wonderful ideas and a lot of feelings to share. However, in the interest of our time limitations, we need to move on."
- "It wouldn't be appropriate for me to give my solutions to your situation. Only your solutions will work for you." After the session, offer her a list of helpful resources.

When Someone Dominates

Set limitations on a person who dominates the group by talking too much and giving too many details. Some possible responses:

- "I can see you have a lot to say on the subject. Because of our time limitations, could you help us focus on the main idea?"
- "Could you summarize so that we can give everybody a chance to speak?"
- Put your hand on her shoulder. "That subject would be a good conversation to continue after the session with others who are interested. You may even want to go out for coffee and discuss it then. For now, we do need to stick to the agenda."

When Someone Blames

Suggest a change of emphasis for the person who is blaming someone else for her pain (e.g., husband, boss, child).

- Focus on her feelings. "How do you feel about what's happening?" Help her name her own feelings.
- Suggest that she take some action. "What steps have you taken to answer your own needs? How do you want to change the situation?"
- Acknowledge that you have heard the feelings, then suggest she look for experienced help. "Sounds like you have a lot of feelings about that. You may need to look at those with someone who can be objective."

Part 2

Session Outlines

Introduction to Session Outlines

The session outlines are designed to help a team of three facilitators and others on the Core Team to lead the eight weeks of MOMS. Facilitators follow step-by-step instructions for each session, leading the group through discussion of each topic.

The outlines assign portions of the session to each facilitator, allowing all three members of the team the opportunity to co-facilitate. In many sections, the directions contain suggested words for facilitators to use in explaining a concept. Remember to adapt the outlines to suit your own team. Reassign roles if necessary. Use your own words. Be yourself. Share answers from your own *MOMS: A Personal Journal.*

Each outline begins with a preparation page and concludes with a reflection page. After completing your own *Journal,* turn to the facilitator's preparation page for the session and fill in the area entitled "At Home." It is essential that each team member comes to the planning meeting with this completed.

As seen in the previous chapter, the Staff Liaison holds the first meeting with the team of facilitators to discuss the purpose of the MOMS and to help the team clearly define its role. Thereafter, facilitators need to meet each week to plan the upcoming session. Many groups have found it helpful to allow for two planning meetings before the first session, to clarify the team plan and to strengthen the team's self-confidence.

Planning Meetings

Schedule each facilitator planning meeting to last 1½ hours. Consider arranging childcare for young children so that the facilitator team can concentrate without interruption.

The following is a possible sequence of events:

- Begin with a prayer. Use the opening prayer from the session you are planning, to help set the tone for the meeting.

- Review any issues or concerns from the previous session. Refer to your journaling notes, if necessary.

- Read the key concepts for the next session. Key concepts are divided into Process and Content. "Process" refers to the group interaction and bonding that you are encouraging. "Content" refers to the particular theme of the week and offers the most important points you would like the group to discuss.

- Practice each section as you read through the whole session. Roleplay each assigned task, using your own words. Make notes on small cards to insert in your journal.

- If one person is uncomfortable with her assigned task, make adjustments to suit the team members' skills.

- Evaluate whether or not the timeline is appropriate for each section. Make adjustments to fit the needs and pace of the group. Remember, some topics are so pertinent to the lives of women that discussion could be lengthy. Make notes in the margin of any areas where you may need to move the group along. Do not read instructions from the book.

- Close with the Closing Prayer for the session.

- Allow a few minutes for each person to write notes on her journal page in this book.

- Confirm the time and place of next week's planning meeting. Check the Things to Remember list on the preparation page.

- Alert the Staff Liaison to any concerns. Use the assessment tool in *MOMS: Developing a Ministry*, Appendix B, if you feel one of the participants needs to be referred to the Staff Liaison.

Preparation Checklist
for Session 1

Staff Liaison

☐ copies of *Called and Gifted* (see Resources section in Part 4). Note that in 1995 the National Conference of Catholic Bishops released a new edition, titled *Called and Gifted for the Third Millenium.* The study guide in Appendix B was written to accompany the original edition of *Called and Gifted;* if you receive copies of the new edition, you will have to adapt the study guide.

Guardian Angel

☐ crate/storage box for storage of materials

☐ name tags, reusable at all eight sessions

☐ pencils in box for easy storage

☐ box/basket for drawing names

☐ cash box for fees, if applicable

☐ tape recorder with a selection of meditative music tapes

☐ attendance list, pre-typed, with eight-week check in

☐ *MOMS: A Personal Journal,* one per participant, distributed in advance

☐ blackboard or easel with paper

☐ chairs in a circle

☐ highlighter pens

☐ file folder for forms from Appendix B

Prayer Leader

☐ small round table for center of room

☐ tablecloth, light color or white

☐ one large candle to light each week

☐ matches

☐ small votive candles, one per person, for Session 2

☐ glass bowl with water for Session 3

☐ serenity prayer card for Session 4

☐ butterfly magnets for Session 5

☐ copies of *Called and Gifted* (see note to Staff Liaison above)

☐ poster board and dry markers for Session 8

☐ glass bowl with water for Session 8

☐ box of tissues

Preparation Page for Session 1:
Self-Esteem and Self-Acceptance

At Home

Read through "Session 1: Self-Esteem and Self-Acceptance" in *MOMS: A Personal Journal.* As you read the text, ask yourself, "What choices have influenced my self-esteem? How have I come to accept myself? Where am I on my path? What does grace mean to me? How has God helped me on my journey?" As a facilitator, you will share these answers with the group.

Notes: _____

_____

At the Planning Meeting

Begin with "Called to Become." Then read through the Session Outline, making sure each facilitator's role is clear. Encourage each facilitator to speak in her own words, even when a suggested text is provided. Practice any sections that seem complicated. Use the space below to note any changes or reminders.

Notes: _____

_____

After the Planning Meeting

Record here your feelings and perceptions relating to the team. Note and pray about any lingering concerns.

Notes: _____

_____

Things to Remember

1. Prepare nametags and attendance sheet.
2. Prepare a basket for drawing names.
3. Refer to Job Descriptions and List of Tasks.
4. Guardian Angel: Prepare to tell your own story of your pathway to self-acceptance.
5. Team: Prepare to share a brief example from your own lives of a "grace-filled moment."
6. Team: Bring copies of "What to Expect" (Appendix B).

Session 1:
Self-Esteem and Self-Acceptance

Key Concepts

Process

Hospitality: Team provides a warm, welcoming environment.

Group Expectations: Team helps participants feel at ease by describing the group learning process, using personal examples.

Content

Self-Esteem: The choices we make influence our self-esteem.

Self-Acceptance: Self-acceptance is a central component of self-esteem. Self-acceptance may take years of practice.

Grace: A special virtue, a gift or help given to a person by God.

Timeline

Time	Person	Task
5	Team	Welcome
10	PL	Prayer
15	P	Ice Breaker
10	Team	What to Expect
10	P	Understanding Self-Esteem
10	P	Group Discussion
10	GA	Pathway to Self-Acceptance
10	GA	Small Group Discussion
10	Team	God's Grace
10	Team	Small Group Discussion
10	PL	Closing Prayer
5	GA	Drawing Names
5	Team	Preparations for next week

Total Time: 2 hours

Key to abbreviations:
PL = Prayer Leader
P = Presenter
GA = Guardian Angel

Team
(5 minutes)

Welcome

Each team member introduces herself and tells why she is here and what she hopes to get out of the eight weeks.

"I am here because..."

"I hope to give and receive..."

Prayer Leader
(10 minutes)

Opening Prayer

See Prayer Ritual (page 83) for preparation.

Presenter
(15 minutes)

Ice Breaker

Ask participants to pair off and spend five minutes sharing numbers 3 and 4 on pages 2–3 in the *Journal*. When the group has returned to the circle, go around the room, asking each person to introduce the person she interviewed. Record numbers 3 and 4 on board.

When finished, draw their attention to the wealth of giftedness in the room. Comment on how in the past our parents may have discouraged us from drawing attention to our strengths. In this group we will help each other see our talents and gifts more clearly.

Team
(10 minutes)

What to Expect in the Group

Use your own words to emphasize the major points from the Welcoming Letter and "What to Expect" list, which they received a week ago. Each team member picks out one or two points to highlight from "What to Expect" (Appendix B).

Prayer Leader
(3 minutes)

Reminder: Use your own words.

"As prayer leader, I will be inviting you to participate in a variety of prayer rituals. I encourage you to respond to the invitation in your own way. Only you know what you want to do and what you want to say. To grow, each person may choose to try out some new behaviors and express ideas and feelings in new ways. To allow each person an orderly turn, I will start with one person in the group and just go around the circle. If you do not wish to pray out loud, you can say 'I pass' or you can say your prayer silently and then squeeze the hand of the person next to you. We will then move on to the next person."

Guardian Angel **(2 minutes)**	"This experience is a support group model for continued education and growth. Each adult is responsible for her need to be comfortable in the process. If you need to stand, stand; if you need a drink, help yourself; if you have a question, ask it, so you will get the most out of being in the group." Give directions on location of bathrooms and any details about childcare.
Presenter **(10 minutes)**	***Understanding Self-Esteem*** Invite participants to turn to page 8. Read aloud and highlight the second paragraph. Comment on what you learned about yourself by writing in your journal. (It is important that you talk about yourself so that participants become comfortable in talking about themselves.) The next key concept to emphasize is that our self-esteem is greatly influenced by the choices we make. We have no control over many circumstances of our lives, but we do have control over our choices.
(10 minutes)	Turn to page 10. Read aloud, "Let's view..." to the end of the paragraph. Invite participants to highlight, then turn to page 11 and share with the same partner as before the two choices they made and how those choices influenced their self-esteem. If there is time, model the activity by sharing an example from your life.
Guardian Angel **(10 minutes)**	***Pathway to Self-Acceptance*** Place the words "Choices" and "Self-Acceptance" under each other on the board. Then say (using your own words), "We have just seen that self-esteem is influenced largely by the choices we make. Self-esteem is influenced also by our acceptance of our true selves and of the gifts that God gave us. Learning self-acceptance is a life-long process." Turn to *Journal* page 14. Give personal examples of where you are on the journey. For example, for self-awareness, you might say, "For me, my first step was simply attending the first MOMS session." For self-respect, "I learned that I did not have to continue carrying the negative messages from my family of origin." Tell your own story of how you are moving in small stages in different areas of your life to complete self-acceptance. Each team member needs to be honest about her own journey, so she can listen and model accepting where she is right now.

Guardian Angel **(10 minutes)**	***Group Discussion of Self-Acceptance***

Ask participants to share with their partner from *Journal* page 13. Let them know they have five minutes to share. You will need to watch the time.

Call everybody back to the large group and invite each person to share where she is on the path right now. Record key concepts on the board. Point out that during the six sessions, we will be able to help each other on the path.

Team **(10 minutes)**	***Mini-Lecture: Seeing God's Grace in the Picture***

Turn to page 15 in *Journal.* Read and highlight first paragraph. Each team member shares a brief personal experience of a "grace-filled moment" in her life. By your simple, practical examples, you can help the group to see how God's grace is an ever-present spiritual energy.

Help them to get in touch with the unconditional love, goodness, and sacredness of the "innermost self." The self is sacred, in spite of all or any negative past experiences. God's grace is within us in each daily happening.

Team **(10 minutes)**	***Small Group Discussion***

Break into pairs to discuss *Journal* page 16. Emphasize the grace, wisdom, or strength they are praying for today because they will be invited to share this in the closing prayer.

Prayer Leader **(10 minutes)**	***Closing Prayer***

See Prayer Ritual (page 84) for preparation.

Guardian Angel **(5 minutes)**	***Drawing Names***

Pass around a basket containing each person's name and phone number. Each person takes a name (not her own). Encourage them to pray for that person and to call each other during the week. It helps to share perceptions about today's experience.

Team **(5 minutes)**	***Preparations for the Next Session***

Ask participants to read and reflect on "Session 2: Stress, Worries, and Anxiety," *Journal* pages 19–40, and to complete the Stress Management Survey before coming to the next session. Show them the scale on page 35. Remind them that they will be using their answers during the session. Encourage them to continue writing in their journals so as to get the most out of the group.

Guardian Angel

"We would like to schedule a friendship social evening at one of your homes after the second or third session. This will be a chance for your spouse or special friend to meet the group. If anyone is willing to be the hostess and invite us into your home, see me after the session. All the hostess has to do is provide her home—a place to gather. The guests will sign up to bring appetizers and refreshments. Be sure to pray for each other during the week."

Reflection Page after Session 1:
Self-Esteem and Self-Acceptance

Complete this page before your next planning meeting.

Note here your observations from the session and any feelings about the participants that you would like to bring to the attention of the team (e.g., a participant who seemed especially shy or sad).

My observations: _____

_____

_____

Did we create a prayerful environment for sharing? Yes No

Did we discuss the key concepts? Yes No

Write here any perceptions relating to your presentations or those of the other facilitators. Note successes so that you can learn to affirm others; note weaknesses so that you can plan improvements or use new techniques.

My perceptions: _____

_____

_____

Suggested changes: _____

_____

_____

How did facilitating this session stimulate my own spiritual growth? What special skills and strengths am I developing?

_____

_____

_____

Preparation Page for Session 2:
Stress, Worries, and Anxiety

At Home

Read through "Session 2: Stress, Worries, and Anxiety" in *MOMS: A Personal Journal.* After reading the text, clearly define your own stress area on the Stress Management Survey. Identify what you do for your own personal renewal. Record one resolution you have already made about stress reduction. Your realistic examples are key to motivating other mothers to be practical and honest.

Notes: _____

_____

At the Planning Meeting

Begin with the Scripture reading from the *Journal.* Share what touched you. Review your Facilitator's Reflection Page from last time for observations, perceptions, or changes. Read through the Session Outline, making sure each facilitator's role is clear. Encourage each facilitator to speak in her own words, even when suggested text is provided. Practice any sections that seem complicated. Use the space below to note any changes or reminders.

Notes: _____

_____

After the Planning Meeting

Record here your feelings and perceptions relating to the team.

Notes: _____

_____

_____

Things to Remember

1. Call participants to get feedback from Session 1 (see Job Description and List of Tasks).
2. Prepare votive candles.
3. Confirm preparations for the Friendship Social.
4. Prepare names for name drawing (cut up a networking list).
5. Hand out corrected networking list.

Session 2:
Stress, Worries, and Anxiety

Key Concepts

Process

Feedback: The team needs to know what the group experienced at the last session before going on.

Content

Stress: Stress is the conflict between our values, our needs, and our expectations.

Guideline 1: Define the area of stress.

Guideline 2: Self-Care: Protection from stress.

Stress Survey: Pick one area to change.

Prayer: Daily prayer is a choice and may reduce stress.

Timeline

Time	Person	Task
10	GA	Welcome
15	PL	Prayer
15	P	Review
15	GA	Areas of Stress
15	P	Self-Care: Small Groups
20	Team	Stress Management Survey
20	PL	Prayer
10	Team	To Take Home

Total Time: 2 hours

Guardian Angel
(10 minutes)

Welcome

As the participants gather, begin to play the Name Game. Each woman says her name with an adjective that helps others remember her name (for example, "I am Paula and I am playful"). As she says her own name, each says the names of those who have already introduced themselves. Example: "I am Anne and I am animated, and this is Terrific Teresa, and that is Playful Paula." Be sure they are wearing nametags so the game is not stressful. The last person to introduce herself will say everybody's name.

Introduce this session, using Key Concepts from previous page. Use your own words. You may want to write on the board.

Prayer Leader
(15 minutes)

Opening Prayer

See Prayer Ritual (page 85) for preparation.

Presenter
(15 minutes)

Review and Feedback

Help participants to recall last week's experience by saying,

"To complete this review, we would like to hear what was most helpful or what most touched you about the last session. Let's just quickly go around the group." Team members begin; be brief.

After all have spoken, briefly review the following concepts from last week, saying "Last time we began to be more aware of our 'real self' and how we esteem our real self":

- We reached out to touch the hand of the person sitting next to us—to be open to the flow of energy between us.
- We said aloud what we liked about ourselves—the unique gift God gave to each of us.
- We began to look at our current position on the pathway to healthy self-esteem and to commit to choosing behaviors that honor that inner self.
- We became aware of the grace-filled moments in our lives and resolved to use this new awareness to make healthy choices every day.

Guardian Angel
(15 minutes)

Areas of Stress

"We will continue to get to know each other by looking at Guideline 1 on *Journal* page 22, defining your highest areas of stress. We will complete this sentence: The two areas of stress in my life right now are…"

Remind participants that the group will respect them if they say, "Today I am feeling that I need to pass." Team members begin by giving clear, specific answers from their own journals. One member records responses on the board. The other two team members help each person clarify her area of stress.

Presenter
(15 minutes)

Self-Care: Protection from Stress

Invite participants to break into groups of two. Ask them to open their *Journal* to Guideline 2 on pages 23–25. Say that one of the ways to show care for the inner, valuable self is to protect ourselves from stress. Share your own answers from questions 1–3 on page 25. Ask participants to share their own answers with their partner. Each partner has three minutes in which to share. Call time halfway through, then again at the end.

Return to large circle. Invite each person to share one thing that she does for self-care. If there is enough time, write these on the board under the title, Self-Care: Protection from Stress.

Presenter
(20 minutes)

Discussion:
Stress Management Survey Results

Leader invites each person to share her lowest score on the Stress Management Scale. Record these on the board under the title, Highest Stress Areas. Call attention to the number of people that have the same areas of high stress. Break into twos or threes and discuss the areas with the lowest scores. Ask them to discuss the question:

Is there anything you can do to reduce stress in that area, or do you need to learn to cope with something you cannot change?

Help each other make one resolution to do one thing next week to reduce stress. Emphasize making one small change at a time. If you try to make too many changes at once, it tends to be self-defeating.

Suggest to participants that they re-read Guidelines 3 and 4 (*Journal* pages 25–27) to see how MOMS is designed to help them handle stress.

Prayer Leader
(20 minutes)

Closing Prayer

See Prayer Ritual (page 86) for preparation.

Guardian Angel
(5 minutes)

To Take Home

Make the following announcements:

"_____ has volunteered to have the friendship social at her home. She brought a map and _____ will help you organize what each person/couple may bring.

"The date and time of our friendship social are as follows: (*Give them the necessary information*)."

Presenter
(2 minutes)

Preparations for the Next Session

Read and reflect on "Session 3: Everyday Spirituality," *Journal* pages 41–50.

Be sure to complete The Sacred in Daily Life: A Meditation, pages 42–43.

Share your sense of spirituality on page 47, and Seeing Motherhood as Ministry on page 49. We will be sharing your ideas.

This is a good time to mention that from here to the end of the sessions, each person's commitment to the group is very important. The trust that is beginning to grow among the participants may be adversely affected if even one person fails to come regularly. (Participants often find it helpful to learn that a casual decision not to show up one week affects the whole group, not just themselves.)

Draw names. This week, call that person to meet for coffee, get together in the park, go for a walk, or just let her know you are praying for her.

Mark your calendar for the Friendship Social.

Prayer Leader
(3 minutes)

"Use your votive candle at least once a day. Ask your children or family to join you at times of stress around your Christ Candle to pray together. Some like to use it for family morning or evening prayer. Children love candles and rituals."

Reflection Page after Session 2:
Stress, Worries, and Anxiety

Complete this page before your next planning meeting.

Note here your observations from the session and any feelings about the participants that you would like to bring to the attention of the team (e.g., a participant who seemed especially shy or sad.)

My observations: _____

_____

_____

Did we create a prayerful environment for sharing? Yes No

Did we discuss the key concepts? Yes No

Write here any perceptions relating to your presentations or those of the other facilitators. Note successes so that you can learn to affirm others; note weaknesses so that you can plan improvements or use new techniques.

My perceptions: _____

_____

_____

Suggested changes: _____

_____

_____

How did facilitating this session stimulate my own spiritual growth? What special skills and strengths am I developing?

_____

_____

_____

Preparation Page for Session 3:
Everyday Spirituality

At Home

Read through "Session 3: Everyday Spirituality" in *MOMS: A Personal Journal.* As you read the text, ask yourself, "How can I talk about my spirituality using ordinary words and everyday experiences?" Come prepared to share definitions of your own spirituality and your ministry. Use your own words.

Notes: _____

_____

At the Planning Meeting

Begin by sharing your own answers to "My Sacred Self." After each has shared her answers, the others say what they heard about God as she spoke. (Example: "God is being revealed in Jozette's smile," or "God's love is being revealed in her three-year-old's hugs.") Then, read through the plan, making sure each facilitator's role is clear.

Notes: _____

_____

After the Planning Meeting

Record here your feelings and perceptions relating to the team. Note and pray about any lingering concerns.

Notes _____

_____

Things to Remember

    1. Holy water for prayer ritual.

    2. Confirm arrangements for Friendship Social.

    3. Prepare names for name drawing.

Session 3:
Everyday Spirituality

Key Concepts

Process

Listening: The team models reflective listening, both to others and to our own inner experiences.

Content

Spirituality: The Whole Spiritual Person wheel helps us to see that spirituality is the central energy for our everyday activities.

Personal Experience: Each person has a unique experience of her own spirituality.

Ministry: Ministry flows out of our spirituality and involves a balance of self and others in everyday tasks and responsibilities.

Choices: Our choices affect our spirituality.

Timeline

Time	Person	Task
10	GA	Welcome
20	PL	Opening Prayer: Meditation
15	P	Whole Spiritual Person
20	PL	Spirituality: Experiences
20	GA	Spirituality: Definitions
20	P	Mom's Ministry
10	PL	Closing Prayer
5	GA	Preparations for the Next Session

Total Time: 2 hours

Guardian Angel **(10 minutes)**	***Welcome*** Ask each person to comment on how the last session helped them deal with stress. Introduce this session from the Key Concepts.
Prayer Leader **(20 minutes)**	***Opening Prayer: The Sacred in Daily Life*** *See Prayer Ritual (page 87) for preparation.*
Presenter **(15 minutes)**	***Whole "Spiritual" Person*** Review the Whole Spiritual Person diagram in the *Journal*, page 45. Help your participants connect this diagram with the questions and answers in the opening prayer. "We often have a tendency to think of our spirituality as a separate piece of the pie. Rather, spirituality is the center of utter goodness, which flows out into the different areas of our life. It is important to nurture the inner spirituality by attending to the healthy balance of these different areas of your life. It helps to think of the center of the circle as the axis of a wheel. If the wheel is uneven—perhaps an area such as the social or the physical is not being attended to—the axis cannot function smoothly." Begin with an example from your own life. Each team member shares one brief example of an area where she has started to keep a better balance. For example, "I have started to see how sacred my body is" or "I now appreciate how important it is for me to take ten minutes to read each day." Use practical, concrete examples from your own life. Ask each person how they can better keep their spiritual wheel in balance.
Prayer Leader **(20 minutes)**	***A Mother's Spirituality*** Invite participants to stay with the same partner they shared with in the opening prayer, and to read the definitions of spirituality, *Journal* page 46. Prayer Leader shares with the group her own responses to the questions on page 46 in the *Journal*. Make it brief while being true to your own experience. Invite the participants to do the same in partners. Remind them there is no "right" or "wrong" to this; they simply need to be true to their own experience.

**Guardian Angel
(20 minutes)**

My Spirituality

"Now that you have shared your experiences since becoming a mother, share what you have written on page 47 in your *Journal.* Each of us will change our definition of spirituality several times in a lifetime, based on our experiences and our changing roles."

Guardian Angel begins by sharing her definition:

My sense of spirituality is_____

_____

_____

_____

Invite each person to read aloud her own answer to the whole group.

**Presenter
(20 minutes)**

Seeing Motherhood As a Ministry

Using your own words, say,

"Just as we have defined spirituality from our own experiences of the sacred, we are now going to look at ministry. Ministry might be described as the actions we take in response to the sacred we see in others and in ourselves."

Participants change partners. Using their responses to the questions on the bottom of page 48 and the top of page 49 in their journals, ask them to discuss:

How do you share your gifts with others?

How do others share their gifts with you?

Allow ten minutes in the small groups and then call them back to the large circle.

Each team member then shares her own definition of ministry from the bottom of page 49.

My ministry is _____

_____

_____

_____

Invite each participant to share a prepared definition of her own ministry. Summarize and thank each person for sharing her personal experiences.

Prayer Leader
(10 minutes)

Closing Prayer

See Prayer Ritual (page 88) for preparation.

Guardian Angel
(5 minutes)

Preparations for the Next Session

Draw names. Encourage participants to pray for and call each other during the week.

Read "Session 4: Feelings." Do all activities.

Mark your calendars now for the Celebration of New Beginnings. Give date and details.

Go to lunch, see a movie, or get together for coffee with someone from the group.

Reflection Page after Session 3:
Everyday Spirituality

Complete this page before your next planning meeting.

Note here your observations from the session and any feelings about the participants that you would like to bring to the attention of the team (e.g., a participant who seemed especially shy or sad.)

My observations: _____

_____

_____

Did we create a prayerful environment for sharing? Yes No
Did we discuss the key concepts? Yes No

Write here any perceptions relating to your presentations or those of the other facilitators. Note successes so that you can learn to affirm others; note weaknesses so that you can plan improvements or use new techniques.

My perceptions: _____

_____

_____

Suggested changes: _____

_____

_____

How did facilitating this session stimulate my own spiritual growth? What special skills and strengths am I developing?

_____

_____

_____

Preparation Page for Session 4: Feelings

At Home

Read through "Session 4: Feelings" in *MOMS: A Personal Journal*. What is the most difficult feeling for you to express? What gets in the way of your expressing that feeling? Recall a time when you chose to take an adult "Time Out." What has helped you the most in learning to express your feelings?

Notes: _____

_____

At the Planning Meeting

Begin with the Serenity Prayer. Then, read through the Session Outline, making sure each facilitator's role is clear. Encourage each facilitator to speak in her own words, even when a suggested text is provided. Practice any sections that seem complicated. Use the space below to note any changes or reminders.

Notes: _____

_____

After the Planning Meeting

Record here your feelings and perceptions relating to the team. Note and pray about any lingering concerns.

Notes: _____

_____

Things to Remember

1. Serenity Prayer cards.
2. Invitations for Celebration of New Beginnings (to be handed out by the Coordinator of Celebration).
3. Time limitations! This topic, feelings, could be a whole six-week course.
4. Hand out list of local resources to participants (prepared by Staff Liaison).
5. Hand out "Time and Talent Form" (Appendix B).

Session 4:
Feelings

Key Concepts

Process

Awareness: The team helps participants become more aware of the inner energy that feelings hold. From awareness flows the desire for new communication skills.

Content

Feelings: Feelings are a gift given to us by God. All feelings, whether expressed or not, have an energy and a creative power.

Behavior: How we express our feelings is a learned behavior.

Relearning: We can choose to learn and practice new behaviors.

Timeline

Time	Person	Task
5	GA	Welcome
5	PL	Opening Prayer
15	GA	Activity
25	P	Feelings as Energy
30	PL	Feelings Flow Chart II
20	P	Time-Out Process
10	PL	Closing Prayer
10	GA	Preparations for Next Week

Total Time: 2 hours

**Guardian Angel
(5 minutes)**

Welcome

Introduce this session, using the Key Concepts. You may want to write them on the board.

"Have you noticed any changes in your attitudes or behaviors since you started this group? Change can be frightening to many people, especially if the change is imposed from the outside. Today we will look at changes we make based on energy coming from inside ourselves."

**Prayer Leader
(5 minutes)**

Opening Prayer

See Prayer Ritual (page 89) for preparation.

**Guardian Angel
(15 minutes)**

Introductory Activity

Break into small groups. Ask them to share their answers on pages 52–53 in their journals. Ask them to listen carefully to the two questions on page 53. Give them five minutes per person. Call time!

Return to the large group. Put answers on the board so that the group can begin to identify (1) the blocks to expression of feelings and (2) the specific feelings that are difficult for this group to express. Say, in your own words,

"You have just taken some of the first steps in a process of understanding your feelings."

**Presenter
(25 minutes)**

Presentation: Feelings As Energy

Ask participants to turn to Feelings As Energy in their *Journals*. Look at Flow Chart I on page 55.

Make the following introductory comments: Feelings are energy. Stress that the expression of this energy is a learned behavior. Some of us have learned excellent ways of expressing our feelings; others realize that we have blocks to overcome before we can release the energy contained within us.

Point out an example of the energy flow from the diagram. You might say something like,

"Imagine that you have a feeling of love for someone. You take a risk and express that love. Your energy may create a whole new, deeper relationship. On the other hand, if you choose not to express that love (perhaps fear of rejection gets in the way), your energy has resulted in undeveloped potential." Illustrate with a personal example from your notes on page 55.

Break the group into partners to discuss their answers to both questions on page 55 of the *Journal*. Give five minutes for each person. Call time!

Return to the large circle. Invite participants to report what gets in their way when they do not express their feelings. Mention that fear may be what gets in the way. The Feelings Flow Chart II will help look at that.

Prayer Leader
(30 minutes)

Feelings Flow Chart II

Invite the group to turn now to the Feelings Flow Chart II on page 57 of the *Journal*.

"People commonly choose *not* to express feelings that are considered unpleasant, in the mistaken belief that this is for the best. However, as you can see on the flow chart, these unexpressed feelings can lead to anxiety, frustration, shame, and guilt."

Give an example from your own experience to illustrate Feelings Flow Chart II.

"Let's break up into twos now so you can share your experience of a specific time when you did express feelings of being hurt or rejected. Answer the first question on page 56 in your *Journal*. Each partner has five minutes."

After they have completed that exercise, invite them to stay with the same partner and share a specific time when they did *not* express feelings of being hurt or rejected. Answer the last two questions on page 56. Same timeframe: each partner has five minutes.

When this is completed, generate a short discussion (five minutes) among the whole group (without rearranging chairs). Emphasize that each person chooses the how, when, and where to express their feelings. It is a real skill to know how, when, and where to communicate.

Presenter
(20 minutes)

Time Out — Not Just for Kids

Invite participants to turn to Time Out — Not Just for Kids on page 59 of the *Journal*. Spend a few moments going through the process a person may take when relearning to express feelings. This will be most effective if you use an example from your own experience to illustrate the steps. The following seven steps summarize *Journal* pages 59–61.

1. The incident occurs.
2. You identify the feelings.
3. You react or respond.

4. You ask for or take time out.

5. You seek clarification as necessary.

6. You sift, weigh, examine, and choose.

7. You specify what you choose to change or will negotiate.

Staying in the large group, leader asks:

How is this process helpful to you at this time in your growth?

Record their answers on the board.

Make one small resolution as a result of today's session.

Prayer Leader
(10 minutes)

Closing Prayer

See Prayer Ritual (page 89) for preparation.

Guardian Angel
(10 minutes)

Preparations for the Next Session

Read and do the activities in "Session 5: Personal Growth," *Journal* pages 63–74.

It is important to continue talking to someone about your feelings. Emphasize the value of sharing these concepts with a friend outside of the class.

"Feelings need to be respected. It is important to learn to respect our own feelings so we learn how to respect others' feelings. If, after this session or any of the sessions, you experience uncomfortable feelings that surface because of the sharing, it is important that you write these out in a journal or talk them through with a trusted friend, a professional counselor, or a spiritual director."

Hand out list of local resources.

Confirm dates of upcoming events.

Reflection Page after Session 4:
Feelings

Complete this page before your next planning meeting.

Note here your observations from the session and any feelings about the participants that you would like to bring to the attention of the team (e.g., a participant who seemed especially shy or sad.)

My observations: _____

_____

_____

Did we create a prayerful environment for sharing? Yes No

Did we discuss the key concepts? Yes No

Write here any perceptions relating to your presentations or those of the other facilitators. Note successes so that you can learn to affirm others; note weaknesses so that you can plan improvements or use new techniques.

My perceptions: _____

_____

_____

Suggested changes: _____

_____

_____

How did facilitating this session stimulate my own spiritual growth? What special skills and strengths am I developing?

_____

_____

_____

Preparation Page for Session 5: Personal Growth

At Home

Read through "Session 5: Personal Growth" in *MOMS: A Personal Journal*. Pick one specific area in your life where you have changed an attitude or behavior. Name one friend who supported you in making that change. List the steps that were necessary for you to make the change.

Notes: _____

_____

At the Planning Meeting

Begin with "For the Friendship of True Women." Then read through the Session Outline, making sure each facilitator's role is clear. Encourage each facilitator to speak in her own words, even when a suggested text is provided. Practice any sections that seem complicated. Use the space below to note any changes or reminders.

Notes: _____

_____

After the Planning Meeting

Record here your feelings and perceptions relating to the team. Note and pray about any lingering concerns.

Notes: _____

_____

Things to Remember

1. Butterflies for closing prayer.
2. Distribute participant evaluation forms to be collected at Session 8.
3. Remind participants of the RSVP date for the Celebration of New Beginnings.
4. Team begins to prepare certificates for Celebration (see Appendix B and page 70).
5. Notify the Staff Liaison of time and place of the planning meeting for Session 8.
6. Be prepared to receive and distribute gifts from prayer partners.

Session 5:
Personal Growth

Key Concepts

Process

Change: The team helps participants look at areas for personal growth and choose one area to change.

Content

Soul Time: A period of reflection or private time every day is essential for personal growth.

Growth: Mental health requires being attentive to personal growth.

Friends: Others can help us in choosing small steps.

Small Steps: Take one small step each day and respect your own inner pace (Butterfly Prayer).

Timeline

Time	Person	Task
5	GA	Welcome
15	PL	Prayer
15	P	Icebreaker
30	GA	Discussion
25	P	Small Group Sharing
20	PL	Closing Prayer
10	GA	Preparations for Next Week

Total Time: 2 hours

Guardian Angel
(5 minutes)

Welcome

Make an announcement about upcoming events. Review "Feelings" from Session 4 (optional). Introduce this session, using the Key Concepts.

Prayer Leader
(15 minutes)

Opening Prayer: "For the Friendship of True Women"

See Prayer Ritual (page 91) for preparation.

Presenter
(15 minutes)

Ice Breaker: How Do I Find "Soul Time?"

To participate fully in these group sessions, you have had to structure quiet reading and journaling time at home these past few weeks. Presenter shares how she manages to find "soul time" each day. Be honest. Then say,

"Let us discuss how you manage to make time for yourself in the course of a busy day. Turn to the person next to you and exchange your strategies."

Give them five minutes.

Return to large group. Invite each woman to briefly share how she takes time for herself.

Guardian Angel
(30 minutes)

Discussion

Break up into new groups of two to share the statement that you circled on page 68 or 69 and what you rewrote after "I wish I could ..." from page 69 in the *Journal.* Give each woman five minutes to share. Call time at the end of each five minutes.

Mention that each person has the power within herself to change a wish into a choice.

Return to the large group.

Invite them to share with the whole group which statement they have chosen to work on.

Invite each person to read her statement in her own words. Affirm each woman for her ability to choose an area of growth for herself.

Presenter
(25 minutes)

Small Group Sharing

"Now that we have each chosen an area to work on, we will help each other clarify the first steps."

Invite them to break into twos again and help each other with the steps each one wants to take in order to make a change in her attitude or behavior. Give them this example:

B. "I wish I could express my own thoughts."
    1. Slow down and clarify for myself what I really think.
    2. Give myself permission to say what I really think.
    3. Share my thoughts with a trusted friend.
    4. Pick the time and place to express my thoughts.
    5. Ask God for the strength to do this.

Important point: This example demonstrates that making any change in an attitude or behavior is a step-by-step process, and others may be able to help us to clarify the steps.

**Prayer Leader
(20 minutes)**

Closing Prayer: "The Butterfly"

See Prayer Ritual (page 91) for preparation.

**Guardian Angel
(10 minutes)**

Preparations for the Next Session

Read "Session 6: Expressing Values in Friendships" and "Postscript: Beyond Session 6," pages 75–90 in the *Journal*.

Complete all activities.

Hand out evaluation forms. Encourage them to be aware of the importance of taking time to evaluate and turn it in before the celebration. Confirm plans for Celebration of New Beginnings.

Set definite time and place to discuss continuation. Mention the Continuing the Journey worksheet, which will be provided next week to help them decide what to do next.

Reflection Page after Session 5: Personal Growth

Complete this page before your next planning meeting.

Note here your observations from the session and any feelings about the participants that you would like to bring to the attention of the team (e.g., a participant who seemed especially shy or sad.)

My observations: _____

_____

_____

Did we create a prayerful environment for sharing? Yes No

Did we discuss the key concepts? Yes No

Write here any perceptions relating to your presentations or those of the other facilitators. Note successes so that you can learn to affirm others; note weaknesses so that you can plan improvements or use new techniques.

My perceptions: _____

_____

_____

Suggested changes: _____

_____

_____

How did facilitating this session stimulate my own spiritual growth? What special skills and strengths am I developing?

_____

_____

_____

Preparation Page for Session 6:
Expressing Values in Friendships

At Home

Read through "Part 6: Expressing Values in Friendships" in *MOMS: A Personal Journal*. Ask yourself:

What friendships have helped me to express my values?

_____

How does my daily behavior express my true values?

_____

Soul values give us each courage and inspire us to be valiant women. How am I already a valiant woman?

_____

At the Planning Meeting

Begin by naming the three people who have influenced your development. Read the Prayer Reflection by Miriam Therese Winter. Then read through the Session Outline, making sure each facilitator's role is clear.

Notes: _____

After the Planning Meeting

Use this time to prepare Certificates of Achievement On a separate sheet, record your impressions of each participant's special gifts. Complete your facilitator's evaluation and schedule a meeting with Staff Liaison.

Notes: _____

Things to Remember

1. Collect the participants' evaluations.
2. Last-minute reminders for the Celebration of New Beginnings.
3. Hand out the "Personal Discernment" and "Continuing the Journey" worksheets as well as a copy of *Called and Gifted* with its Study Guide and the Vatican Council II Fact Sheet (see Appendix B).
4. Inform participants that their prayer sponsors have been invited to Session 7.
5. Confirm with Staff Liaison planning meeting for Session 8.
6. Prepare Certificates of Achievement to be given out at Session 7.

Session 6:
Expressing Values in Friendships

Key Concepts

Process

Self-Validation: The team helps each participant name her values and her gifts.

Content

Values: Values are in our true self, and they are revealed in our relationships.

Friendships: Clarifying and expressing values are key components of friendships. Value clarification is a long and sometimes painful process that requires honesty and fidelity to the relationship.

Valiant Woman: Inside each of us is a valiant woman. Friends help us to claim our inner resources and strengths.

Timeline

Time	Person	Task
5	GA	Welcome
15	PL	Prayer
30	P	Relationship Values
20	PL	Discussion
20	GA	What Needs to Be Done?
15	PL	Closing Prayer
15	GA	Announcements
5	P	Prayer Sponsors

Total Time: 2 hours

**Guardian Angel
(5 minutes)**

Welcome

Invite each person to comment on the steps from the last session, *Journal* page 70. Were they able to take one step toward a new behavior? Introduce this session, using the Key Concepts.

**Prayer Leader
(15 minutes)**

Opening Prayer

See Prayer Ritual (page 93) for preparation.

**Presenter
(30 minutes)**

Values in Friendships

Turn to Values in Friendships on page 78 of the *Journal*. Break into diads and have them dialogue about the three values that are present in a specific friendship, as recorded on page 80. Begin by giving your own three values. Give them ten minutes. At the end of five minutes, let them know they have five minutes left.

Return to the whole group. State that when we talk about our values, we learn about our true self. Ask each person what she learned about herself as she did this activity, as recorded on page 80 in the *Journal*. Write key phrases on the board.

**Prayer Leader
(20 minutes)**

Discussion

Ask the group:

As you reread the values on pages 78–79, which one are you struggling with the most in a specific relationship?

What gets in your way as you try to express that value?

Refer them to their answers on pages 80–81.

Remind participants to center the discussion on what is causing the difficulty in each of them. We each can speak only from our own perspective. Facilitators bring up from their experience an occasion of a friendship or relationship where there was a difficulty caused by one person's values not being a high priority for the other. For example,

"Equality is a value I am trying to develop in a friendship. I do not see myself as equal to my friend, and I often give in to her ideas and suggestions. In doing so, I give her more respect and dignity than I do my true self. I wish I could respect my own ideas and feelings as equal to hers."

Guardian Angel
(20 minutes)

What Do I Need to Do?

Make it clear to the group that there are steps we need to take in order to learn to express our own values.

1. Clearly define what gets in your way.
2. Clearly image what concrete behavior would express your value in the way that you want to.
3. Start to practice those skills and that behavior slowly until you are comfortable with the skills and the new behavior.

Finish this discussion by going around the group, asking each person to share their answer to the second question on page 81:

How would I like to express that value?

Begin by sharing your own answer: _____

_____

_____

Prayer Leader
(15 minutes)

Closing Prayer

See Prayer Ritual (page 93) for preparation.

Guardian Angel
(15 minutes)

Announcements

"We have come to the end of six sessions. You are invited to continue to grow in your spirituality, in the awakening of all the possibilities within you. Next week, there will be an evening of celebration for these new beginnings."

Hand out the "Personal Discernment" and "Continuing the Journey" worksheets. Ask them to bring the completed worksheets to Session 8. Hand out copies of *Called and Gifted* and the accompanying Study Guide and the Vatican Council II Fact Sheet. Invite participants to read the document, then jot down the practical applications in their lives as mothers. Hand out the "Time and Talent Form," to be collected at the Celebration of New Beginnings.

Remind them to bring completed evaluations to Session 8.

Presenter
(5 minutes)

Suggest that participants sit with their prayer partners at the Celebration and share their experience of the past six weeks. During the program that evening, there will be a time when they can thank their prayer sponsors for their support.

Reflection Page after Session 6: Expressing Values in Friendships

Complete this page before your final facilitator meeting.

Note here your observations from the session and any feelings about the participants that you would like to bring to the attention of the team (e.g., a participant who seemed especially shy or sad.)

My observations: _____

_____

_____

Did we create a prayerful environment for sharing? Yes No

Did we discuss the key concepts? Yes No

Write here any perceptions relating to your presentations or those of the other facilitators. Note successes so that you can learn to affirm others; note weaknesses so that you can plan improvements or use new techniques.

My perceptions: _____

_____

_____

Suggested changes: _____

_____

How did facilitating this session stimulate my own spiritual growth? What special skills and strengths am I developing?

_____

_____

_____

Use these reflections to assist you in completing the Facilitator Team Feedback Form.

Confirm the time, place and date for your team evaluation meeting.

Session 7:
Celebration of New Beginnings

Introduction

The Celebration is a two- to three-hour gathering, involving a sit-down, shared meal, a featured speaker, and affirmation of leaders and participants.

For some participants, the MOMS sessions may have been their first involvement in a church setting. They may be members of the church, but without any adult experience of participation and involvement. The Celebration of New Beginnings provides an opportunity for the MOMS participants to see the connection between the six weeks they have just experienced and the larger church community of which they are a part. By inviting key leaders of the church to attend and even speak at this celebration, the MOMS Core Team helps strengthen the link to the larger community.

Responsibility

The Coordinator of Celebration of New Beginnings supervises a group of peers who plan, provide, and evaluate this community event. See job description for tasks (Appendix A).

Timing

The Celebration typically takes place within a week of the sixth session. It is often held in the evening, although lunchtime celebrations have worked out at many locations. The Celebration is an occasion where MOMS participants can concentrate on their own desire to grow; therefore, spouses are not usually invited. The Core Team makes this decision. Some groups have invited spouses; others have made this a family event.

Important Considerations

Purpose. Keep the purpose of the celebration in mind as you do all your planning. The primary aims are:

1. To affirm the women who have chosen to devote time and energy to their own personal growth and to the personal growth of others.

2. To provide a casual social experience that reinforces the connection of the MOMS to the church community.

3. To expose the participants to resources for continued support or education within the community (guests, community leaders, speakers, handouts, etc.)

4. To connect all mothers in the community with each other.

Invitations. Invitations (Appendix B) may be simple and inexpensive and should include:

1. Date, time, and place (map if needed).

2. Agenda & featured speaker. State topic.

3. Cost and RSVP. (Include phone number for RSVP and whom to make checks payable to.)

Room Arrangement. Have a hospitality table by the door, and some instrumental music playing in the background. Provide an appetizer table with simple hors d'oeuvres and a non-alcoholic punch. Have centerpieces or tasteful table decorations on all tables. Lighting from table lamps provides a softer setting than ceiling lights. To maintain a good flow of conversation, place no more than four or five people at a table. Avoid having a head table. Seating arrangement is key if you have the celebration in a room at a restaurant. Conversation is difficult when there are six or more people at a table.

Shared meal. Since women usually have the task of preparing and serving the family meal, this celebration offers an opportunity for them to sit down and be served. Arrange for the food to be prepared and served by a caterer, a women's guild, a senior group, or past MOMS participants. Ask for volunteer table servers from youth ministry.

Hospitality. Make sure somebody welcomes each person upon arrival, gives each a name tag (preferably with name already written), leads guest to an appetizer table, and introduces guest to others. This often requires two people.

Welcome. The assigned M.C. makes opening comments, introduces any guests, and gives an outline of the evening's events.

Opening Prayer. Design a type of ritual that gathers and welcomes all of the people to participate in the celebration. The type of ritual will depend on the nature or needs of the group and the guests, and the liturgical season. A prayer ritual for this celebration is provided in the Prayer Ritual section.

Icebreaker or Community-Building Activity. This activity may take place at the beginning of the evening or during dessert. Choose an activity in which people will have a chance to talk to somebody they don't already know. Allow fifteen to twenty minutes for this activity.

Invited Speaker. Choose a speaker with care. Make sure the speaker understands that this is a personal and spiritual growth group, not a Mom-and-Tot group, a play group, or a social club. (The use of the term MOMS can be deceiving to some.) Be clear in writing about the exact time, place, topic, and stipend. Have the speaker approved by the Staff Liaison. Alert the speaker that there may be diverse kinds of families represented: single parent, blended families, multi-generational, etc. Some possible topics for a short (20-minute) presentation:

- prayer in the home
- women and spirituality
- small communities of today's church
- Advent activities and spirituality
- Christmas without crisis
- the value of friendship for mental and spiritual health
- resources for ongoing spiritual growth
- Lenten activities: Family Holy Week and Easter Rituals

Certificate of Achievement. The Facilitator team prepares certificates to be signed and presented by the Staff Liaison, Pastor, or Coordinator of MOMS. The certificate may be personalized by using the church or community logo. A sample is in Appendix B. The facilitators decide on the unique gift or talent of each participant and note it on the certificate.

Evaluation. The vitality of this ministry comes from the participation of women in planning, facilitating, and evaluating the learning process. Evaluation is a tool for increasing participation and commitment to a successful ministry. The Staff Liaison picks four or five potential leaders from among the women at the Celebration. She asks them to complete the evaluation form. Their objective comments are valuable and will be used to continue to develop the ministry. A suggested form, which may be adapted to your local setting, is in Appendix B.

Sample Agenda for Session 7:
Celebration of New Beginnings

6:00   Arrival of guests. Hospitality table by entrance, with name-tags (preprinted). Collect any money due.

6:15   Icebreaker activity. Team helps introduce guests to each other.

6:25   Welcome. MC introduces herself and presents the agenda for the evening. She introduces any special guests.

6:30   Opening prayer ritual. See Prayer Ritual (page 95).

6:45   Meal served.

7:15   Dessert mixer. Provide a game or activity that moves people to another table.

7:45   Introduction of guest speaker.

8:15   Presentation of certificates by a staff representative or pastor. Appreciation of team, childcare volunteers, and servers.

8:30   Invitation to upcoming events/calendar of community events. Reminder of Session 8: discussion of *Called and Gifted* and "Discernment: Continuing the Journey." Other announcements.

8:45   Closing prayer. See Prayer Ritual (page 96).

Preparation Page for Session 8:
Discernment: Continuing the Journey

At Home

Read through "Called and Gifted" and note on the Study Guide a practical application in each area of your life.

At the Planning Meeting

Share your practical applications.

Notes: _____

_____

After the Planning Meeting

Use the time to clarify what choices you have to offer to the participants. Complete your facilitator's evaluation and schedule a meeting with the Staff Liaison. Clarify your plans with other facilitators.

Things to Remember

1. Collect the participants' outstanding evaluations.
2. Confirm that the Staff Liaison is coming and has a lesson plan.
3. Collect the "Time and Talent Form."
4. Schedule an evaluation meeting for team and Staff Liaison.
5. Have water on prayer table for closing.
6. Prepare tables with poster board and markers to be used for the *Called and Gifted* activity.
7. Hand out "Group Rules for Ongoing Groups" with a clear message that this is your last session acting as a facilitator with them.
8. Hand out a list of resource materials (obtained from Staff Liaison and/or Coordinator of Resources).

Introduction to Session 8:
Discernment: Continuing the Journey

This session needs to be well planned and timed by the Staff Liaison and Facilitator Team in order to guide each participant toward making a decision about her continued involvement in MOMS activities and her level of commitment to this group. It may be a difficult transition for facilitators as well as participants.

Each participant uses the "Personal Discernment" worksheet to help determine the best choice for her at this time. The Staff Liaison and the Facilitator Team use the *Called and Gifted* activity to help participants see their call to lay ministry and provide a list of resources in the community. Those participants who commit to continuing to meet use the "Continuing the Journey" worksheet to record date, time, place, topic, and facilitator.

The Facilitator Team needs to clearly state their choice not to continue to facilitate this group. Help participants make the transition from having a team of "outside" facilitators to choosing their own books, videos, and topics for continuing the journey. The Staff Liaison and Coordinator of Resources distribute a list of resources in the areas of family spirituality and women's spirituality. The Facilitator Team also hands out the "Group Rules for Ongoing Groups" for successful continuation of the group.

Timing

This session usually takes place a week or two after the Celebration of New Beginnings. The time lapse allows participants to fill out the worksheets and provides the team and Staff Liaison with an opportunity to evaluate the six-week experience and celebration.

Session 8:
Discernment: Continuing the Journey

Key Concepts

Process

Decision-Making: To encourage each woman to make her own decision about her spiritual journey ("Personal Discernment" worksheet) and to clarify her interest in the MOMS ("Continuing the Journey" worksheet).

Separation: To give a clear message that the Facilitator Team will not be facilitating the next session of the group.

Content

Adult Education: Participants discuss *Called and Gifted* as it applies to each individual.

Ministry: Each participant shares her chosen area of ministry/service.

Group Rules: Participants are provided with a set of rules for peer ministry in a group.

Timeline

Time	Person	Task
5	GA	Welcome
10	PL	Prayer
20	P	"Personal Discernment" worksheet
40	Staff Liaison	*Called and Gifted* with Study Guide
20	P	"Continuing the Journey" worksheet, Part I: Involvement in Ministry
10	GA	"Continuing the Journey" worksheet, Part II: Plans for the Future
10	PL	Decision: Silent Reflection and Commitment
5	Team	Appreciation

Total Time: 2 hours

Guardian Angel **(5 minutes)**	***Welcome*** Introduce this session, using the Key Concepts to clarify the objectives.
Prayer Leader **(10 minutes)**	***Opening Prayer*** *See Prayer Ritual (page 97) for preparation.*
Presenter **(20 minutes)**	***"Personal Discernment" Worksheet*** Invite each participant to share her choice about personal development.
Staff Liaison **(40 minutes)**	***"Called and Gifted" with Study Guide*** Briefly give some background about Vatican Council II and its relationship to this document using the Fact Sheet. Divide the group into subgroups. Ask the first group to share their insights and practical applications of question 1 from the Study Guide; the second group to share question 2; and so forth. Give the groups ten to fifteen minutes to prepare a poster, song, or skit that clearly states the essential meaning of their section. After they present their work to the whole group, ask the "audience" to comment on what they liked the best. Summarize what you hear for the group.
Presenter **(20 minutes)**	***"Continuing the Journey" Worksheet, Part I*** Invite each person to share her answers, then hand out fliers about peer ministry training (or whatever facilitator training your community offers).
Guardian Angel **(10 minutes)**	***"Continuing the Journey" Worksheet, Part II*** Invite each person to share her answers, and record them on newsprint. Make it clear that they need to determine their own facilitator for each session. Be sure that all evaluations have been turned in.
Prayer Leader **(10 minutes)**	***Decision: Silent Reflection and Commitment*** *See Prayer Ritual (page 97) for preparation.*
Team **(5 minutes)**	Express your appreciation and your plans for your own continued journey.

Reflection Page after Session 8:
Discernment: Continuing the Journey

Complete this page before your Facilitator Evaluation meeting.

Note here your observations from the sessions.

My observations: _____

_____

_____

Did we create a prayerful environment for sharing? Yes No

Did we discuss the key concepts? Yes No

Write here any perceptions relating to your presentations or those of the Staff Liaison. Note successes and weaknesses. This session needs to strengthen our universal call to ministry. It may be difficult.

My perceptions: _____

_____

_____

Suggested changes: _____

_____

_____

How did facilitating this session stimulate my own spiritual growth? What special skills and strengths do I bring to ministry?

_____

_____

_____

Use these reflections to assist you in completing the Facilitator Team Feedback Form.

Part 3

Prayer Rituals

Introduction to Rituals

> Ritual provides the bridge between inner and outer worlds and creates a context for reconnecting to the seat of our souls. The end result of all ritual is increased balance, strength, energy, and comfort.[1]

We learn about life by taking time to reflect on our experiences. In pausing to reflect on our experiences, we recognize the sacred in them. Certain experiences—celebrations, particularly—stand out in our mind as especially sacred, and we find ourselves repeating them often. They have become traditions.

In the home, families perceive that rituals have grown up around certain seasonal celebrations. At Christmas, for example, the timing of the dinner, the food preparation, and all the special touches unique to each family give to the event a sense of tradition and history that deepens each person's identity within the family. Family members don't like changes in the ritual. They often feel: "That's our special way of doing it. This is sacred to us. It's who we are."

In some homes, the celebration of a birthday may be a tradition, enjoyable but without any sacred overtones for any of the family members. In other homes, siblings and parents may view the occasion as sacred and may be very attached to their own way of celebrating it. This ritual provides an opportunity for them to learn about and deepen their family bond.

Just as the family rituals allow us to perceive who we are, the rituals in the MOMS are designed to lead the participants to a greater awareness of what is happening between them. The opening and closing rituals invite the participants to express in their own words their experience of being in the group. During a session where participants have discussed values and experiences of their past friendships, the facilitator invites each member to pray aloud on behalf of a special friend. A session where participants are encouraged to turn to each other for support contains a prayer that involves them listening to each other.

The ritual, therefore, puts participants in touch with a deeper reality. A lit candle may symbolize each person's inner light, strength, or wisdom. Passing around a lit candle then symbolizes the bonding between the members as they share their light, wisdom, and strength with each other during the session.

The success of the prayer rituals will depend on the subtler rituals that the team has created: the hospitality extended to each participant

---

[1] Excerpted from Angeles Arrien's foreword to *The Art of Ritual*, by Renee Beck and Sydney Barbara Metrick (Berkeley, California: Celestial Arts, 1990), ii.

and the trust that has developed among them as they create a safe place for each other. These experiences help the women participate in the prayer rituals.

The Components of Ritual

The components of ritual are story, symbol, and movement. Through story, symbol, and movement, mutual recognition and affirmation occur.

- **Story:** The stories used in ritual may be the stories from our own life experiences, or stories from Scripture, or myths. Myths are stories that help structure reality for people. They have an emotional content, are timeless, and have a visual character. The Butterfly poem may be regarded as a myth about death and resurrection.

- **Symbol:** The symbols of ritual are never merely objects. They are human representations of hopes and fears, joys and longings. Symbols may be contemporary or traditional. For Christians, the Paschal candle is a traditional symbol of light in darkness.

- **Movement:** The movements of ritual create an opportunity for bonding the participants and allow outward expression of an inner experience. Movement helps participants sense the sacredness of life within and between them. Meditative music helps create an environment where it is easier to recognize the holiness in familiar actions such as passing a candle, holding hands, or touching water. Actions such as letting water flow through one's fingers evoke memories of past experiences with water.

Creating a Sacred Environment

The whole team is involved in creating a sacred environment of quieting down, listening to the music, dimming the lights, and participating in a natural and prayerful manner. In this environment, each woman is invited to pray verbally or non-verbally in the presence of other women.

When preparing to lead a prayer ritual, there are three aspects of the environment to consider:

- **Prepare the room:** The position of the chairs; the amount of lighting; the music (whether instrumental or vocal); the color, texture, and design of the cloth materials; candles; greenery in the prayer space.

- **Prepare yourself:** Center yourself as prayer leader; adapt the rituals to the needs of the participants. Use silence, short words of introduction, pauses.
- **Prepare the participants:** Set up an environment and expectation that they are free to participate in whatever way is comfortable for them. Model the ritual for them so that they feel confident in their ability to participate.

To Ensure Success

1. Prepare small note cards of your directions to place in your *Journal.* Do not read directly from the Prayer Ritual section. Practice aloud at home until you are comfortable with your own words and are able to give clear directions.

2. Invite each person to participate in her own way.

3. Allow plenty of time for each person to freely express herself.

4. Allow silence to be just a few seconds longer than you think is comfortable. This slows the pace, fosters a deeper level of inner quieting, and gives the participants time to integrate directions.

5. Be sure your initial directions are short and simple. Then, clearly demonstrate by example and gesture how to move through the ritual.

6. At the end of each prayer ritual, allow a short period of silence so that all can focus on their response to the prayers.

Rituals for Session 1:
Self-Esteem and Self-Acceptance

Objectives

- To build a sense of trust and acceptance in the group.
- To invite easy verbal or non-verbal participation (e.g., holding hands, saying a prayer).
- To begin prayers of gratitude and petition in a group.
- To invite the participants to a quiet time where they can be reflective and listen to others.

Environmental Preparation

Place chairs in a circle around a prayer table. A prayer table may be a small round table with a plain white or light-colored tablecloth. This table will be in the center of the group at each session.

On the table place a scented white candle or a Christ Candle (a candle with a liturgical symbol on the candle—usually available at religious gift shops). Use the same candle all eight sessions.

Create a prayerful mood using reflective music in the background. It is important to place the tape recorder where you can easily control the volume.

**Opening Prayer
(10 minutes)**

Called to Become

All stand around table.

Read slowly and clearly the psalm "Called to Become" on page 7 in the *Journal*.

When finished, invite them to reach out and take the hands of the women on their right and left. Say,

"I invite you to shut your eyes and concentrate on one thing you are thankful to God for right now. I will begin, and we will go around to the right. If you are not comfortable praying out loud, you can pray silently. When you have finished your silent prayer, you can just squeeze the hand of the person next to you."

After the last woman has spoken, Prayer Leader says, "Amen."

**Closing Prayer
(10 minutes)**

Spontaneous Prayer of Petition

All stand.

Reflective music in the background. Leader may read the following prayer or say it spontaneously:

"God, we have come together today to ask you to open our hearts to a fuller understanding of ourselves and others. Give us the grace to walk our own path to new growth."

Invite each person to ask for some grace for the week ahead.

Encourage each woman to take five to fifteen minutes each day to pray before she does her assignment in the *Journal.*

Rituals for Session 2:
Stress, Worries, and Anxiety

Objectives

- To build trust in God and yourself by taking "time out."
- To invite participation in the prayer candle ritual and encourage its daily use.
- To provide an experience of meditating, reflecting, and sharing scripture.

Environmental Preparation

Use the same table arrangement as in Session 1. For each woman put an individual votive candle in a circle around the Christ Candle with a taper to light the votive candle from the Christ Candle. Each woman will be invited to step forward and take her votive candle to light during the closing prayer ritual.

Prepare yourself before the session by reading Ephesians 3:14–21, *Journal* page 20, aloud twice, with all the feeling you have for the words being proclaimed.

Opening Prayer (15 minutes)

Ephesians 3:14–21

All sit in a circle.

Introduce the prayer by saying in your own words:

"When we read Scripture we are reading the Word of God. When we listen carefully, the Word being read touches some part of our inner being, our true self."

Read St. Paul's letter to the Ephesians 3:14–21 slowly and prayerfully from *Journal* page 20. When finished, invite participants to close their eyes and slowly take several deep breaths so they can feel their "hidden self grow strong." Ask,

"What word, image, or phrase touched you as you heard the Scripture read?"

Begin by telling what word, image, or phrase touched you. Go around the circle. Team begins.

When finished, say:

"We thank you God for the grace of being here together to share your Word. Amen."

**Closing Prayer
(20 minutes)**

Christ Candle Ritual

Lights should be dimmed or off. All stand.

"In this session we have talked about ways to reduce stress. One way is to slow down and turn to God, our inner light and strength."

Ask them to take three deep breaths and meditate on the Christ Candle in the middle of the table. Invite them to pray for the grace to do one small thing to reduce stress this week. Ask them to follow your example by lighting a candle from the Christ Candle and then saying your prayer. Remind them that they can participate by taking a candle with a silent prayer or a verbal prayer. Prayer Leader begins. When all have finished lighting candles, say "Amen."

Assignment

Tell the women that the candle is theirs to take home. Encourage them to light the candle at least once a day or at especially stressful times and pray for Christ's peace for self, family, and other women in the group. They may want to use their candle at family mealtimes.

Rituals for Session 3:
Everyday Spirituality

Objectives

- To create a prayerful listening environment for each other by encouraging sacred silence.
- To invite women to share how they experience God in their daily life.
- To help each person see how sacred her body, mind, feelings, commitments, and relationships are.

Environmental Preparation

Prepare as usual.

**Opening Prayer
(20 minutes)**

My Sacred Self

All sit.

Prepare the participants for a different kind of prayer in this session—listening with care to a prayer-partner talking about her "true self."

Point out the sacred in the ordinary (e.g., beautiful hair, a feeling of peace, love for a child or a spouse, a commitment to helping a bed-ridden neighbor). These things, sometimes, are taken for granted. We often forget each is a sacred part of creation. God pays attention to every last detail of our sacred self.

Say, using your own words:

"Today our prayer is to share with a partner the meditation, "My Sacred Self." Break into groups of two and share how you experience God working in your life, using your answers on pages 42–43 of the *Journal.* One partner will be silent, using her best listening skills to hear God's life in the other. The other partner will be short and specific. No dialogue here. Listening is a prayer form. I will give the signal for you to reverse roles after five minutes."

Give them five minutes each, then call them back to the large circle. Ask each person to quietly think about what she heard *about God* when she listened to her prayer-partner. Participants may need help with this. (A sample response might be: "God's presence was revealed in the joy Maria felt when her son hugged her" or "Joanna's commitment to helping her daughter through Dyslexia reminds me of

God's commitment to us.") Give your own example first. Then, go around the room, asking each for one phrase. Write it on the board.

After sharing, Prayer Leader says,

"God, we have come together to praise and thank you for the way you have created each human being within a sacred body. Open our hearts and minds to recognize the sacred in our daily life, as we care for our whole person and the human needs of those we love. Amen."

Closing Prayer (10 minutes)

Water Ritual

All stand.

When all are standing around the prayer table, wait a few moments to allow them to listen to the meditation music and become centered. Then say:

"Water reminds us that all life comes from God, the creator of land and water. In baptism, water cleansed us as we were invited to the fullness of life in Christ. In our role as mothers, we have given hundreds of drinks, washed countless sticky hands and faces, and bathed many little bodies. We know the sacredness of water. Our closing prayer today invites you to use the water to renew your commitment to the spiritual journey with Christ and ask for the cleansing, nourishment, or refreshment you need on the journey.

"I invite each of you to step up to the water and pray for the grace to move forward into a fuller recognition of the sacredness of your life. Place your hand or hands in the water in any prayerful gesture that is comfortable for you, as you make your petition.

Prayer Leader begins with a simple, direct petition. Ask for one blessing for yourself in words or a silent prayer. Choose a simple gesture (slowly rubbing hands in the water or making the sign of the cross) to model for participants uncomfortable with rituals.

After the last person has finished, Leader says:

"Creator God, we recognize you more fully in our daily tasks and relationships. Help us to become aware of your presence this week. Amen."

Rituals for Session 4:
Feelings

Objectives

- To encourage inner serenity as participants prepare to make small changes.
- To invite usage of a simple daily prayer.

Environmental Preparation

Prepare as usual. Play meditative music (no lyrics) softly in the background. Place small cards of the Serenity Prayer around the candle on the table, for use in the Closing Prayer.

**Opening Prayer
(5 minutes)**

Serenity Prayer

All stand.

Leader says:

"Feelings can be frightening. So can change. The simplicity of the Serenity Prayer has universal appeal. Please close your eyes and take a couple of deep breaths to center yourselves. Reach into your innermost center of energy and draw forth the peacefulness from deep within."

Allow two or three minutes of silence. Slowly read the Serenity Prayer from the *Journal*, page 52.

**Closing Prayer
(10 minutes)**

Serenity Prayer

Gather the group around the prayer table. Ask participants to take a Serenity Prayer card. Give them a few moments to center themselves and to remember their resolution from the last activity. Invite them to read the prayer aloud in unison. Then go around the group, inviting each to share her resolution. End by saying:

"And Christ said to us, 'Where two or more are gathered in my name, there am I in their midst.' Let us go in peace. Amen."

Rituals for Session 5:
Personal Growth

Objectives

- To help women see the sacredness of true friendships and the blessing of being a friend.
- To use a symbol (butterfly) to represent a sacred experience of death and new life.
- To pray for the grace needed for growth.

Environmental Preparation

Prepare as usual. Place a butterfly pin, magnet, or card around the Christ Candle for each woman, in readiness for Closing Prayer.

**Opening Prayer
(15 minutes)**

For the Friendship of True Women

All sit. Ask each person to assume a relaxed position with feet flat on the floor, hands open in lap. Ask them to take three to four deep breaths. Invite them to shut their eyes if it is easier to meditate.

Slowly and prayerfully read "For the Friendship of True Women" from the *Journal*, pages 64–65. When finished, invite each person to share what touched her as you read the prayer-psalm (perhaps a short phrase, a particular word from the text, e.g., "the touch of a sister's hand"). After each has shared, stand and invite each person to pray for any person or situation the psalm brought to her mind. Leader begins by praying for a friend. When all are finished, say, "Amen."

**Closing Prayer
(20 minutes)**

The Butterfly

All stand.

Explain that the butterfly can be seen as a symbol of Christ's death and resurrection. The caterpillar had to "let go" of all her busy little legs and go into the dark cocoon. Only with time and darkness did the butterfly come to birth. Many times, we are frightened of darkness, so we fail to respect the time it takes. Each person's pace is unique and cannot be hurried.

Invite them to hold hands around the Candle while the leader reads "The Butterfly" poem on page 72 of the *Journal*.

Then invite each person to step forward, praying for God's grace to start a new behavior. After her prayer, each picks out a butterfly to meditate on this week. Leader says,

"Put the butterfly in a place where you will be sure to see it, and trust that Christ will give you the energy you need to fulfill your new growth resolution from this session."

Rituals for Session 6:
Expressing Values in Friendships

Objectives

- To invite each woman to thank God for the persons who have blessed her.
- To affirm each person's giftedness with a blessing from others in the group.
- To take time for each person to look at her inner resources and strength as being a valiant woman.

Environmental Preparation

Prepare as usual.

**Opening Prayer
(15 minutes)**

A Prayer Reflection

All sit in a circle.

Ask participants to take a couple of deep breaths, while centering themselves. Prayer Leader slowly reads the Prayer Reflection from *Journal* page 76.

When finished, invite participants to remember one person who has helped her express her true self. Refer to *Journal* page 77. Pause for a few minutes to give them time for reflection. The leader then begins by naming her person and briefly stating what that person gave her.

When finished, say this closing prayer:

"Creator God, we praise and thank you for the power of your presence deep in our hearts and revealed to us in each other. Amen."

**Closing Prayer
(15 minutes)**

A Valiant Woman

All sit. Listen to reflective music in the background.

Prayer Leader introduces the prayer by asking women to sit quietly with hands open on lap. Suggest they close their eyes.

"During the past six sessions we have often been inspired by God's grace working in each person. Now, center yourselves in preparation for the reading, 'A Valiant Woman'. Take a few minutes to meditate on how you too are a valiant woman."

Give the group about two minutes to reflect.

Reader reads "A Valiant Woman" (from Proverbs 31:10–25) on *Journal* page 82 with a spirited pace.

The Prayer Leader continues:

"I invite each woman to name her own gift. Share with us a way in which you have been called to be a valiant woman."

Example: "I thank God for I have been given the gift of perseverance through many changes."

The Prayer Leader begins. Continue around the group until each person has had a chance to speak. Let there be some silence. After the last person has spoken, Prayer Leader says, "Thank you, God, for the gifts we have received."

Pause.

"Let us now stand and extend to each other the Peace of Christ in whatever way is comfortable for you."

Women may choose to shake hands or hug.

Rituals for Session 7:
Celebration of New Beginnings

Objectives

- To celebrate the unity of the group through the symbols of bread and wine.
- To respect the diversity within the group by inviting individual prayer intentions.
- To affirm friendship in the tradition of the Jewish Seder and Christian Holy Thursday.

Environmental Preparations

Arrange for an area where guests can gather in a circle around a prayer space. In the space arrange a candle and a round loaf of bread in an attractive, easy-to-pass basket. Create a prayerful mood by playing meditative music in the background. For the Closing Prayer, have ready a blessing cup with non-alcoholic wine. Assign a person to read at the Opening and Closing Prayer.

Opening Prayer (15 minutes)

Celebration of Friendship

All stand.

Leader gathers the assembly. She begins by saying:

"We have gathered here to celebrate the community we have formed during these six sessions. We are mindful that, since the beginning of history, there are stories of people gathering to break bread, share a meal, and thank God for special blessings. This loaf of bread (hold up loaf) is symbolic of our community. Like the wheat, each of us came as kernels and broke open and shared parts of ourselves. Together, we created this nourishing community."

Reader says:

"Lord Jesus Christ, we come together to praise and thank you. Make us aware of your presence as we eat this food with gratitude and joy. May all that we say be in the spirit of truth and friendship."

Leader says:

"I invite each of you to reflect for a moment on the greatest blessing or grace you have received during the last six weeks."

Pause for two or three minutes to allow a prayerful silence to grow.

"Hold those personal thoughts in your heart. Now, I will pass this loaf of bread around, and invite each person to thank God for a special blessing you received. After your prayer, break off a piece of bread as a symbol of being a part of the whole Christian community."

Leader begins by asking the person on the right to hold the basket. Leader then thanks God for a grace, breaking off a piece of bread. As each person prays, the person to the right assists by holding the basket.

Closing Prayer (15 minutes)

Blessing Cup Ritual

All stand.

Leader says,

"During the Passover celebration, Jesus took the traditional blessing cup and invited his friends to drink and proclaim a blessing of hope for the newly forming community."

Reader lifts the blessing cup and says,

"God, our Creator, bless this cup of friendship. Give to us in this ancient ritual the grace and the courage we need to be faithful on the journey."

Leader takes the blessing cup from the Reader and prays for the grace needed on the journey. (Ask for a specific blessing for yourself so that others will be encouraged to do the same). Drink from the cup, wipe with cloth napkin, and pass to the next person. When all have finished, leader says the closing oration:

"Blessed are you, God, for all the gifts you have given us, but especially we thank you for one another. May we always be united in Christian community. We ask for these blessings in Jesus' name. Amen."

Rituals for Session 8:
Discernment: Continuing the Journey

Objectives

- To set the environment for decision-making, the discernment process, and commitment.
- To respect the diversity of needs, gifts, and decisions within the group by inviting each individual to articulate her needs and decisions at this time.
- To affirm making a commitment and the choice to share it in a group of women-friends.
- To share the facilitators' own decisions about continuing the journey.

Environmental Preparation

Keep it simple. Place a Christ candle and holy water on a table. Use music that will help participants be still and quiet down.

Opening Prayer (10 minutes)

All sit in a circle. Ask participants to take a couple of deep breaths while centering themselves and focusing on the presence of God.

"God, we gather at this time of transition to thank you for what you have given us. Help us to make good decisions and to respect each person's ideas, feelings, and needs. Come, Holy Spirit, fill our hearts and minds with the truth and courage to choose what's best for each of us. Amen."

Invite each person to thank God for whatever special grace or benefit she received from being in this group of women.

Closing Prayer (15 minutes)

Decision: Silent Reflection and Commitment

All sit in silence and listen to reflective music in the background for about five minutes. Then invite each one to share what she has decided to do for her own continued spiritual development.

Leader stands and, as she verbalizes her plans to continue her journey, approaches the water. Use any appropriate gesture. Invite others to do the same.

When finished, ask the appointed new facilitator to announce the time, place, and topic for the next session.

Resources for Rituals

We have included this annotated bibliography of resources for rituals for those who want to understand more about rituals and develop the skills of leading others in prayer.

Beck, Renee, and Sidney Barbara Metrick. *The Art of Ritual: A Guide to Creating and Performing your own Rituals for Growth and Change*. Berkeley, California: Celestial Arts, 1990. The "Ten Guidelines for creating your own Rituals" and the "Ritual Worksheet" are the most practical aspects of this book for any person beginning rituals. Background information on understanding the process of ritual provides excellent foundational material for appreciating the significance of ritual in spiritual growth.

Boyer, Ernest Jr. *Finding God at Home: Family Life as Spiritual Discipline*. San Francisco: Harper & Row, 1984. An excellent book on family spirituality. Contains many ideas on simple family rituals appropriate for younger children. At the end are short services for beginning and ending each day.

Cunningham, Nancy Brady. *Feeding the Spirit: How to Create Your Own Ceremonial Rites, Festivals, and Celebrations*. San Jose: Resource Publications, Inc., 1988. Contains 24 ceremonies you can celebrate in your own home. Ceremonial rites such as Dream Making, Color Meditation, and Moon Magic are designed to help the reader turn ordinary, daily events into special moments that will nourish the spirit.

Curran, Dolores. *Traits of a Healthy Family*. New York: Ballantine Books, 1983. Excellent practical ways to develop 15 healthy traits in the family. Chapter eight, which discusses "Tradition and Ritual," emphasizes building and maintaining a healthy functioning family through tradition. Many ideas on how to preserve a sense of tradition and celebration in all kinds of families at all stages of development.

Driver, Tom F. *The Magic of Ritual*. New York: Harper Collins, 1991. A scholarly resource for those who want to understand and create rites of passage and ceremonies of healing, grieving, and celebration.

Finley, Mitch and Kathy. *Christian Families in the Real World: Reflections on a Spirituality for the Domestic Church*. Chicago: Thomas More Press, 1984. Only one chapter out of ten is about family ritual, but its eight pages give many good basic ideas and lots of encouragement for beginners.

Hays, Edward M. *Prayers for the Domestic Church*. Easton, Kansas: Forest of Peace Books, Inc., 1979. Contains a wide variety of simple but well-written prayers appropriate for many everyday situations and events. Designed specifically for use in the home.

_____. *Family Prayers and Ritual*. Kansas City, Missouri: National Catholic Publishing Co., 1985. Two audiocassette tapes. Excellent. Easy to understand and readily applicable to a family.

Hughes, Kathleen, RSCJ. *Lay Presiding: The Art of Leading Prayer*. Collegeville, Minnesota: The Liturgical Press, 1991. Written for leaders who want to learn the art and science of presiding. They may be parents learning to bless their children, leaders at group meetings, a hostess wanting to lead invited guests in prayer, or a church member presiding at an evening of prayer. Contains prayers of praise, thanksgiving, reconciliation, and hope. Short and clear.

Kelley, Gail. *Traditionally Yours: Telling the Christian Story through Family Traditions*. San Jose: Resource Publications, Inc., 1987. Contains personal accounts from those involved in establishing traditions that incorporate

Christian values and attitudes. Readers learn how to turn everyday events and big events into family traditions and faith experiences.

Lord, Dr. Frank. *Stories They'll Remember: Teaching your Children through Stories*. Loveland, Ohio: Treehaus Publications, 1990. A short, easy-to-read book on communicating age-appropriate values to children through stories. A must for every parent.

Mackintosh, Sam. *Passover Seder for Christian Families*. San Jose: Resource Publications, Inc., 1986. The traditional seder prayers of the Passover meal are presented in a Christian context for celebration at home. Includes complete directions, food recipes, prayers, and an introduction to the seder meal and its Jewish origins. Adaptable for church use.

Nelson, Gertrude Mueller. "When Heaven and Earth Become One." *Praying* (March-April 1989): 18-25. Nelson states, "We are by our very nature spiritual persons seeking wholeness. Ritual and celebration reveal God and our spirituality right in the midst of the ordinary, everyday life." This article gives several practical examples.

_____. *To Dance with God*. New York: Paulist Press, 1986. One of the best on family and community celebrations. Introductory material is brief but beautifully written. Most of the book is practical family celebrations and rituals for the church year.

Padovano, Anthony. *Love and Destiny: Marriage as God's Gift*. New York: Paulist Press, 1987. A practical, poetic book written from a theologian's perspective. Chapter five discusses the importance of rituals and memories in marriage.

Paladin, Lynda. *Ceremonies for Change: Creating Personal Ritual to Heal Life's Hurts*. New Mexico: Stillpoint Publishing International, 1991. An excellent resource to help people and groups rediscover the patterns that empower them. Paladin presents rites, rituals, ceremonies, and celebrations as a symbol of change. She suggests creative imagination, free-spirited play, and spontaneous whimsy as a way to add renewed spiritual energy to the tasks of daily living.

Robinson, J., and Jean Staehli. *Unplug the Christmas Machine: How to Have the Christmas You've Always Wanted*. New York: William Morrow, revised edition 1991. These two women have helped thousands of families, singles, and children learn to enjoy the holidays, deal with their anger at the commercialization of holy days, and plan concrete ways to maintain sanity and sacredness in heart, home, and community.

Schaffran, Janet, and Pat Kozak. *More than Words: Prayer and Ritual for Inclusive Communities*. New York: Crossroads, revised edition 1988. Emphasizes inclusive language, symbols, images of God, and cultural pluralism. Includes prayers and 29 prayer services.

Sears, Marge. *Life Cycle Celebrations for Women*. Mystic, Connecticut: Twenty-Third Publications, 1991. An excellent book of 19 clearly prepared rituals for pregnancy, miscarriage, transitions, and a variety of relational experiences. It emphasizes the need for a circle of support and empowerment between women of all nations. Includes readings, songs, and resources.

Travnikar, R. *The Blessing Cup: 24 Simple Rites for Family Prayer Celebrations*. Cincinnati: St. Anthony Messenger Press, 1979. A valuable resource containing scripture-based blessing cup rituals for home and small groups.

To Celebrate: Reshaping Holidays and Rites of Passage. Georgia: Alternative Press, 1987. This is a collection of celebrations and rituals for those who are not satisfied with the models of celebration offered by our consumer society. A guideline and resource for creating rituals that encourage respect for the environment and enhance human relationships.

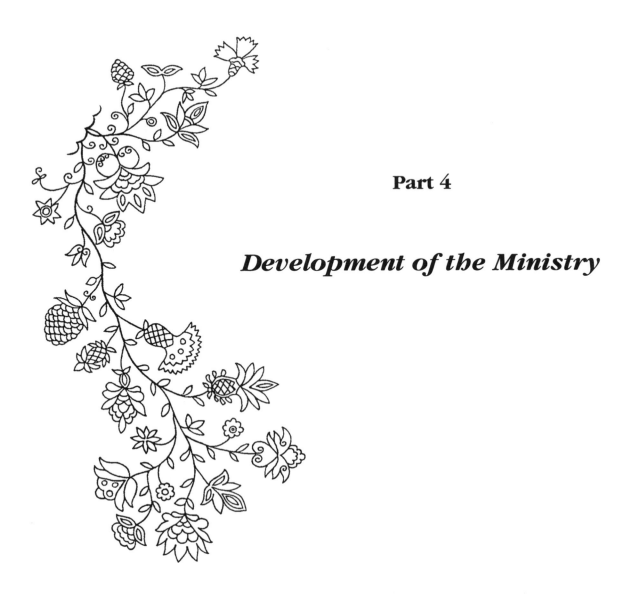

Part 4

Development of the Ministry

Evaluation

Evaluation is an essential part of effective leadership and ministry. It is part of a feedback loop between participants, staff, and pastoral leadership. Leaders who make decisions without feedback or input from the participants tend to be less effective in their planning.

Evaluation is also a crucial part of the adult learning process. By reflecting on the merits of the experience, participants have a chance to relive portions of the past six weeks and assess the practical implications of the topics they have discussed.

Evaluation Forms

Evaluation forms need to be simple, clear and related to the stated goal of the session. The MOMS uses three evaluation forms to obtain feedback (see Appendix B):

- **Participants' Evaluation Form.** Participants complete this at home after the fifth session, finish it, and hand it in after the sixth session.

- **Celebration of New Beginnings Evaluation.** Certain guests/participants are chosen to evaluate this evening and mail back the completed form.

- **Facilitator Team Evaluation Form.** Each facilitator completes this two-sided form.

Recommendations

After receiving the evaluations, the Core Team summarizes each set of evaluations and decides on recommendations for changes. The team prepares a written report for future planning and for review by the Staff Liaison. The Coordinator may receive suggestions indicating a need for major areas of change (for example, the establishment of an adequate childcare ministry, the allocation of a budget for the ministry, or improved resources). There are certain areas that are not within the Staff Liaison's or Coordinator's power to change, but it is appropriate to send a memo to the person who may be able to initiate change.

The effectiveness of the evaluation tool is its ability to assist in the communication process by providing adequate data for the feedback loop. The sample forms in Appendix B may be used as they are or adapted to the specific needs of your community.

Making Referrals

A critical component of the Ministry of Mothers Sharing is the provision of resource materials. Most participants want to continue their growth, both personally and, for some, as part of a group.

Many enjoy and wish to continue the experience of affirming each other in their ministry of motherhood. Some want to develop skills of nurturing a Christian family or discover within themselves a need for parenting classes. Others seek further development of leadership skills that may have emerged during the MOMS sessions. Some want to learn to share their faith with other adults and need guidance in how to articulate their experience of God. Others become aware that they have some personal issues that they now have the confidence to deal with. During Session 4, participants receive a list of community resources prepared by the Staff Liaison. For most women, this is all they need.

There are some instances when the Staff Liaison and the Facilitator team may choose to minister to the participants of the group by making a specific referral. There are two directions for referral: to professional services outside the immediate community, and to ongoing support and growth programs or ministries within the church community.

Professional Referrals

Occasionally facilitators find that in the group there is a participant who needs the help of a professional or someone more specialized in personal issues. This may be a grief counselor, a minister or priest, family therapist, financial planning specialist, or school psychologist. When this happens, special care and delicacy are crucial. A referral is not a simple matter. The person and the assessment of facts require careful handling, otherwise the participant may feel judged and will not follow through in seeking and obtaining the resources she needs.

An Assessment Tool for Referral is provided in Appendix B as a resource for the facilitators. The team of facilitators informs the Staff Liaison that one of the participants seems to need a referral. Based on the information in the Assessment Tool for Referral, the Staff Liaison takes the responsibility for assessing the situation and making the referral as needed. The following are good guidelines for a Staff Liaison when making professional referrals:

- Evaluate the participant's readiness for referral. Remember that she must see the need for referral. It is unwise to "sell" the participant on the need for help. If she is not ready to seek help, then she is unlikely to follow through, though she may express intentions of doing so.

- Determine together what resources best match the needs of the situation. Implementing this guideline presupposes that you have a prepared written list of resources and that you have some familiarity with the specialized services they provide. Share all the relevant information with the participant so that she can make an informed choice.

- Respect the participant's right to self-determination as you explore the possible options, but offer your recommendation as to which resource is likely to be most beneficial. Remember, the initiative in making the appointment resides with the participant.

- Avoid making false promises or conveying unrealistic reassurance about what another agency can do in assisting the participant. Affirm her in her ability to check out whether the agency fits her needs. Emphasize the skills she has displayed in the MOMS and how she will use them to share her ideas, problems, feelings, and needs as she searches for the services she needs.

- Alert her that each person and agency has its own methods, policies, and procedures. Avoid specifying what the professional or agency will accomplish. If you prescribe what other practitioners should do, you impose a handicap upon them and set the participant up for disappointment.

Community Referrals and Empowerment in Ministry

The process of spending six weeks in the company of other women who support them in their growth often helps participants to clarify the areas where they have skills, special interests, or leadership potential. With an invitation from the Staff Liaison or the facilitators, these skills can be further developed.

The Staff Liaison and the Core Team of MOMS have a crucial role to play in the area of referrals. By its commitment to continued growth and by making resources available, the staff provides a genuine opportunity for people who have just experienced the trust and empathy of a small group to become integrated into the life and resources of the church community.

The steps to appropriate referral and empowerment of participants are:

1. Provide a tool, such as the Time and Talent form in Appendix B, for participants to assess their own needs, gifts, or leadership skills.

2. Make available to participants (through the Coordinator of Resources) information on all ongoing adult education, faith formation, and other ministries of the church and local community.

3. Gather all the completed Time and Talent or assessment forms from participants.

4. Personally invite each participant to pursue an area of interest or service indicated by her responses on the form.

Options

Some possible options to make available to ongoing groups or individuals are:

- **Facilitator training.** Support groups hoping to remain together can avoid many pitfalls when facilitators are trained and have ongoing opportunities to develop their skills.

- **Lay Ministry seminar.** Since Vatican II, it has become important to teach the theology of Lay Ministry. A seminar may be helpful to shift participants' image of ministry from a parent- child image to an adult-to-adult image. This experience includes training in communication skills and group dynamics.

- **Adult faith formation courses.** The safe, non-threatening environment of the MOMS often awakens in participants a desire to learn about their faith and their church traditions. This is an ideal time to encourage ongoing faith formation for individuals and couples, especially if the course is offered in a small-group style.

- **Parenting classes.** The MOMS often surfaces in participants the need to improve communication skills within the family. A course on parenting, which they may take with their spouse, may be a necessary step.

- **Family Spirituality.** Some women want to learn how to make religious traditions and rituals a regular part of their home life. Workshops based on the liturgical seasons (Advent, Christmas, Lent, Easter, and Ordinary Time) are particularly helpful.

- **Small faith-sharing communities.** In congregations which have committed to restructuring around these groups, also known as Small Basic Christian Communities, an entire MOMS group may choose to become a faith-sharing group.

- **Service to the community.** Individuals usually need help in discerning where they can put their skills to best use. Outreach to the community through ministries such as St. Vincent de Paul, Rainbows for All God's Children, Ministry of Separated and Divorced, etc., are possible avenues. Healthy ongoing groups realize that service is an essential component of the Christian lifestyle.

- **Classes on leadership in ministry.** Innovative church communities often provide these for people who enjoy the challenge of developing themselves and others and who are not afraid to lead.

Resources

The following pages contain books, programs, and audiovisual materials that are helpful for groups seeking ongoing development in a variety of areas. Those most often used by MOMS groups are designated with **.

Discussion Programs

**These booklets are available from Sheed and Ward, P.O. Box 414292, Kansas City, MO 64141-4292 (Tel: 1-800-333-7373). Each booklet contains material suitable for group discussion over a six- to twelve-week period.

> Gallagher, Maureen. *Spirituality of Parenting.* 1985.
> Head, Mary E., and Janet A. Galligan. *Women, Work and Gospel Values.* 1988.
> Riley, Maria. *In God's Image.* 1985.
> ———. *Women Faithful for the Future.* 1987.
> Schwartz, John C. *God's One Family.* 1990.
> Simcik, Joanne. *Lenten Journey.* 1990.

**Available from Paulist Press (993 Macarthur Boulevard, Mahwah, NJ 07430) from the Madeleva Lectures Series:

> Boys, Maru C. *Jewish-Christian Dialogue.* 1997.
> Cahill, Lisa Sowle. *Women and Sexuality.* 1992.
> Chittister, Joan. *Job's Daughters: Women and Power.* 1990.
> Collins, Mary. *Woman at Prayer.* 1987.
> Dreyer, Elizabeth. *Passionate Women: Two Medieval Mystics.* 1989.
> Harris, Maria. *Woman and Teaching.* 1988.
> Hayes, Diana L. *Hagar's Daughters: Womanist Ways of Being in the World.* 1995.
> Hellwig, Monika K. *Christian Women in a Troubled World.* 1985.
> Johnson, Elizabeth J. *Women, Earth, and Creator Spirit.* 1993.
> Leckey, Dolores R. *Woman and Creativity.* 1991.
> Rodriquez, Jean. *Stories We Live.* 1996.
> Schneider, Sandra M. *Women and the Word.* 1986.

Available from Harper (151 Union Street, Suite 401, San Francisco, CA. 94111, Tel: 1-800-328-5125):

> **Kidd, Sue Monk. *When the Heart Waits: Spiritual Direction for Life's Sacred Questions,* 1990.
> **May, Gerald G., MD. *Addiction and Grace: Love and Spirituality in the Healing of Addictions,* 1988.
> **Sanford, John A. *The Kingdom Within: The Inner Meaning of Jesus' Sayings,* 1987.
> **Wiederkehr, Macrina. *A Tree Full of Angels: Seeing the Holy in the Ordinary,* 1988.

Available from St. Mary's Press (702 Terrace Heights, Winona, MN. 55987):

**Bergan, Jacqueline Syrup, and Marie Schwan. *Take and Receive Series.* 1985. Based on the Ignatian exercises, each of these five books is an excellent basis for group discussion and theological reflection.

For Private Reading or Group Discussion

Angelou, Maya. *The Heart of a Woman.* New York: Bantam Books, 1981.

Bankson, Marjory Zoet. *This Is My Body: Creativity, Clay, and Change.* San Diego: LuraMedia, 1993.

Barkley, Elizabeth Bookser. *Loving the Everyday: Meditations for Moms.* Cincinnati: St. Anthony Messenger Press, 1996.

———. *Woman to Woman: Seeing God in Daily Life.* Cincinnati: St. Anthony Messenger Press, 1998.

**Belenky, Mary; B. Clinchy; N. Goldberger; and J. Tarule. *Women's Ways of Knowing: The Development of Self, Voice and Mind.* New York: Basic Books, 1986.

Bergan, Jacqueline Syrup, and Marie Schwan. *Taste and See.* Winona, Minn.: St. Mary's Press, 1996.

**Berrien Barends, Polly. *Gently Lead: How to Teach Your Children about God While Finding Out for Yourself.* New York: HarperCollins, 1991.

Borton, Joan C. *Drawing from the Women's Well: Reflections on the Life Passage of Menopause.* San Diego: LuraMedia, 1992.

Boyer, Ernest, Jr. *Finding God at Home: Family Life As Spiritual Discipline.* San Francisco: HarperSanFrancisco, 1991.

Buechner, Frederick. *Telling Secrets.* New York: HarperCollins, 1991.

Called and Gifted for the Third Millennium: Reflections of the U.S. Catholic Bishops on the Thirteenth Anniversary of the Decree on the Apostolate of the Laity *and the Fifteenth Anniversary of* Called and Gifted. Washington, DC: United States Catholic Conference, 1995. (Tel: 1-800-235-8722).

**Cameron, Julia. *The Artist's Way.* [PLACE:] J P Tarcher, 1992.

Cappacchione, Lucia, PhD. *The Well-Being Journal.* Van Nuys, Calif.: New Castle Publishing Co., 1989.

Carnes, Robin Deed, and Salley Craig. *Sacred Circles: A Guide to Creating Your Own Women's Spirituality Group.* San Francisco: HarperSanFrancisco, 1998.

**Chittister, Joan D. *Heart of Flesh: A Feminist Spirituality for Women and Men.* Ottowa, Ontario: Novalis, 1999.

———. *Wisdom Distilled from the Daily.* San Francisco: HarperSanFrancisco, 1991.

Coffey, Kathy. *Experiencing God with Your Children.* New York: Crossroads, 1997.

Curran, Dolores. *Stress and the Healthy Family.* San Francisco: Harper & Row, 1985.

———. *Traits of a Healthy Family.* San Francisco: Harper & Row, 1983.

———. *Working with Parents.* Circle Pines, Minn.: American Guidance Service, 1989.

DeGidio, Sandra. *Enriching Faith Through Family Celebrations.* Mystic, Conn.: Twenty-Third Publications, 1989.

Doyle, Brendan. *Meditations with Julian of Norwich.* Santa Fe: Bear & Co., 1983.

Duerk, Judith. *Circle of Stones: Woman's Journey to Herself.* San Diego: LuraMedia, 1989.

Durka, Gloria. *Praying with Julian of Norwich.* Winona, Minn.: St. Mary's Press, 1989.

Eadie, Betty J. *Embraced by the Light.* Placerville, Calif.: Gold Leaf Press, 1992.

Finley, James. *The Contemplative Heart.* Notre Dame: Sorin Books, 2000.

Finley, Mitch. *Your Family in Focus: Appreciating What You Have, Making It Even Better.* Notre Dame: Ave Maria Press, 1993.

Fitzgerald, William John. *Stories of Coming Home: Finding Spirituality in Our Messy Lives.* Mahwah, N.J.: Paulist Press, 1998.

Gately, Edwina, VMM. *I Hear a Seed Growing.* Trabuco, Calif.: Source Books, 1990.

————. *Psalms of a Laywoman.* Trabuco, California: Source Books, 1988.

————. *A Warm Moist Salty God: Women Journeying Towards Wisdom.* Trabuco, Calif.: Source Books, 1993.

Girzone, Joseph E. *Joshua.* New York: Collier Books, 1987.

————. *Joshua and the Children.* New York: Collier Books, 1989.

————. *Joshua the Shepherd.* New York: Collier Books, 1990.

Glavich, Mary Kathleen, SND. *Prayer Moments for Every Day of the Year.* Mystic, Conn.: Twenty-Third Publications, 1998.

Harris, Maria. *Dance of the Spirit: The Seven Steps of Women's Spirituality.* New York: Bantam Books, 1989.

Jennett, Vickie LoPiccolo. *MOMStories Instant Inspiration for Matters* (Cycle A). San Jose: Resource Publications, Inc., 1998.

————. *MOMStories: Minute Meditations for Mothers* (Cycle B). San Jose: Resource Publications, Inc., 1999.

————. *MOMStories: Quiet Contemplations for Mothers* (Cycle C). San Jose: Resource Publications, Inc., 2000.

Kidd, Sue Monk. *The Dance of the Dissident Daughter: A Woman's Journey from Christian Tradition to the Sacred Feminine.* New York: Harper & Row, 1996.

Kohlbenschlag, Madonna K. *Kiss Sleeping Beauty Goodbye.* New York: Harper & Row, 1979.

**Lerner, Harriet Goldhor, PhD. *The Dance of Anger: A Woman's Guide to Changing the Patterns of Intimate Relationships.* New York: Harper & Row, 1985.

**————. *The Dance of Intimacy.* New York: Harper & Row, 1989.

Lindbergh, Anne Morrow. *Gift from the Sea.* New York: Pantheon Books, 1986.

Linn, Dennis, et al. *Good Goats: Healing Our Image of God.* Mahwah, N.J.: Paulist Press, 1994.

Linthorst, Ann Tremaine. *Mothering As a Spiritual Journey: Learning to Let God Nurture Your Children and You along with Them.* New York: Crossroad, 1993.

Mayer, S. Suzanne, IHM. *Celebrating the Woman You Are.* Mahwah, N.J.: Paulist Press, 1995.

Meehan, Bridget Mary, SSC. *Exploring the Feminine Face of God: A Prayerful Journey.* Kansas City, Mo.: Sheed & Ward, 1991.

Moltmann-Wendel, Elisabeth. *The Women around Jesus.* New York: Crossroad, 1988.

Pearson, Carol Lynn, *A Widening View.* Salt Lake City: Bookcraft, Inc., 1983.

**Popov, Linda and Dan, and Hohn Kavelin. *The Family Virtues Guide: Simple Ways to Bring Out the Best in Our Children and Ourselves.* Plume, New York: Penguin Books U.S.A., 1997.

Powell, John, S.J. *Happiness Is an Inside Job*. Allen, Texas: Tabor Publishing, 1989.

**Puls, Joan. *Seek Treasures in Small Fields: Everyday Holiness*. Mystic, Conn.: Twenty-Third Publications, 1993.

Ramshaw, Gail. *Words around the Fire*. Chicago: Liturgy Training Publications, 1990.

————. *Words around the Font*. Chicago: Liturgy Training Publications, 1994.

Remen, Rachel Naomi, MD. *Kitchen Table Wisdom: Stories That Heal*. New York: Riverhead Books, 1996.

**Rupp, Joyce. *The Cup of Our Life: A Guide for Spiritual Growth*. Notre Dame: Ave Maria Press, 1997.

**————. *May I Have This Dance?* Notre Dame: Ave Maria Press, 1992.

————. *Praying Our Goodbyes*. Notre Dame: Ave Maria Press, 1988.

————. *Your Sorrow Is My Sorrow: Hope and Strength in Times of Suffering*. New York: Crossroads, 1999.

Sanna, Ellyn. *Motherhood: A Spiritual Journey*. Mahwah, N.J.: Paulist Press, 1997.

Shaevitz, Marjorie Hansen. *The Superwoman Syndrome*. New York: Warner Books, 1984.

Sleevi, Mary Lou. *Women of the Word*. Notre Dame: Ave Maria Press, 1990.

————. *Sisters and Prophets*. Notre Dame: Ave Maria Press, 1990.

Straughn, Harold. *The Five Divorces of a Healthy Marriage*. St. Louis: CBP Press, 1986.

Svoboda, Melannie, SND. *Everyday Epiphanies: Seeing the Sacred in Everything*. Mystic, Conn.: Twenty-Third Publications, 1997.

Swift, Helen Cecilia, and Margaret Telscher. *Unveiling the Feminine Face of the Church*. Cincinnati: St. Anthony Press, 1989.

Thompson, Marjorie J. *Family: The Forming Center. A Vision of the Role of Family in Spiritual Formation*. Nashville: Upper Room Books, 1989.

Wicks, Robert J. *Everyday Simplicity: A Practical Guide to Spiritual Growth*. Notre Dame: Sorin, 2000.

**Wiederkehr, Macrina. *The Song of the Seed: A Monastic Way of Tending the Soul*. New York: HarperCollins, 1995.

**Winter, Miriam Therese. *The Gospel According to Mary: A New Testament for Women*. NewYork: Crossroads, 1994.

Understanding the Development of a Group

Boland, Thomas. *Doing Family Ministry—A Process Approach*. Conception, Mo.: Abbey Press, 1982.

Dass, Ram, and Paul Gorman. *How Can I Help? Stories and Reflections on Service*. New York: Alfred A. Knopf, 1990.

Fisher, Gemma, SNJM, and Marie and David McGee. *Sharing Your Faith: A Formation for Ministry Program*. Kansas City, Mo.: Sheed and Ward, 1987.

Gershon, David, and Gail Straub. *Empowerment*. New York: Bantam Doubleday Dell Publishing, 1989.

Johnson, David, and Frank Johnson. *Joining Together: Group Therapy and Group Skills*. Englewood Cliffs, N.J.: Prentice-Hall, Inc., 1975.

Juliano, Carroll, and Loughlan Sofield. *Collaboration: Uniting Our Gifts in Ministry*. Notre Dame: Ave Maria Press, 2000.

Hammett, Rosine, and Sofield Laughlin, S.J. *Inside Christian Community*. Hartford, Conn.: LeJacq Publ., 1981.

Kirschenbaum, Howard, EdD, and Barbara Glaser, MR. *Developing Support Groups*. San Diego: University Associates, 1978.

Luft, Joseph. *Group Processes: An Introduction to Group Dynamics*. Mountain View, Calif.: Mayfield, 1963.

McKinney, Mary Benet, OSB. *Sharing Wisdom*. Allen, Texas: Tabor Publishing, 1987.

Myers, J. Gordon, SJ, and John W. Lawyer. *A Guidebook for Problem Solving in Group Settings*. Kansas City, Mo.: Sheed & Ward, 1985.

Otto, Herbert, PhD. *Group Methods to Actualize Human Potential*. Beverly Hills: The Holistic Press, 1975.

———. *Fourteen New Group Methods to Actualize Human Potential*. Beverly Hills: The Holistic Press, 1975.

Patton, B., and Ken Giffin. *Decision-Making Group Interaction*. New York: Harper & Row, 1978.

Sofield, Loughlan, et al. *Building Community: Christian, Caring, Vital*. Notre Dame: Ave Maria Press, 1998.

Thero, Cynthia. *Can I Help? A Practical Guide to the Care and Feeding of Volunteers*. Denver: The Source, 1989.

Wilson, Marlene. *The Effective Management of Volunteer Programs*. Boulder, Colo.: Volunteer Management Associates, 1976.

———. *You Can Make a Difference*. Boulder, Colo.: Volunteer Management Associates, 1990.

For Further Faith Development

Baranowski, Arthur. *Called to Be Church*. Cincinnati: St. Anthony Messenger Press, 1988. A complete set of materials for restructuring Catholic parishes into smaller base churches. Video also available.

Cawkwell, David, et al. *At Home with the Word 1991*. Chicago: Liturgy Training Publications, 1991. Sunday Scriptures and Reflections, published annually.

Crossroads of Faith. Mission Hills, Calif.: Benziger Publishing, 1989. A series of six topics for small groups from the Diocese of Jefferson City, Missouri. Can be used over a number of years. Contains a manual and leader's guides for each topic.

Chambers, Kate, and Patricia A. Natali. *The Call of the Prophets*. Kansas City, Mo.: Sheed and Ward, 1990. Booklet contains eight sessions.

Exploring the Sunday Readings. Mystic, Conn.: Twenty-Third Publications, published monthly.

Groome, Thomas. *Christian Religious Education: Sharing Our Story and Vision*. New York: Harper & Row, 1980.

Serendipity Small Group Resources. Littleton, Colo.: Serendipity Co., P.O. Box 1012 (Tel: 1-800-525-9563). The Serendipity Company publishes materials for groups of all types: family, bible study, youth, support, or special needs. They are easy to facilitate, and they offer a Christian perspective on the topics for discussion. Catalog available.

Smith, Pamela. *WomanStory*. Mystic, Conn.: Twenty-Third Publications, 1992.

Audio/Video Resources

Archdiocese of Seattle. *Called to Grow: How Is God Revealed?* Kansas City, Mo.: Sheed & Ward Small Group Resources, 1987. Two 120-minute videos, study booklet, and study guide available. Tel: 1-800-333-7373.

Curran, Dolores. *Overcoming Barriers to Spiritual Growth*. Allen, Texas: Tabor Publishing, 1991. Four thirty-minute segments. Comes with facilitator's guide, which includes discussion questions and activities.

Diocese of Baker, Oregon. *De Sales Program, The*. Los Angeles: Franciscan Communications, 1986. Eight study courses of one-hour video sessions. Excellent program for continued adult spiritual formation using Scripture and theological reflections on sacraments and contemporary Christian issues. Manuals, participant's guide books, and facilitator's guides available.

The Faithful Revolutions: Vatican II in Plain English. Allen, Texas: Resources for Christian Living, 1996. Set of videos—$89.95. Tel: 1-800-822-6701.

Foster, Richard J. *The Challenge of the Disciplined Life*. Elgin, Ill.: David C. Cook, 1988. Eight sessions on video, includes facilitator's guide.

My Soul Proclaims: Voices of Catholic Women. Washington, D.C.: United States Catholic Conference, 1993. Originally aired on NBC-TV, this moving one-hour presentation captures the historical and contemporary contributions of Catholic women in the church and in society. Includes discussion guide.

Oblate Media and Communication Group. Award-winning producers, writers and performers are featured in an outstanding collection of video productions. Write to 5901 West Main Street, Suite A, Belleville, IL 62223-4409. Tel: 1-800-233-4629.

Palisades Home Video. A selection of videos for people of faith. Write to 153 Wavery Place, 6th Floor, New York, N.Y. 10014. Tel: 1-800-229-8575.

Smith, Tim and Julie. *Altared 2000*. Mesa, Ariz.: Troubador Publications, 2000. Audiocassette of music on family spirituality.

———. *Eucharistic People*. San Jose: Resource Publications, Inc., 1993. Audiocassette.

Windows to Understanding. Washington, D.C.: National Conference of Catholic Bishops, 1992. A stimulating documentary on the delicate balancing act many women face in daily life, the stresses women feel when torn between home and work obligations, the significance of older women passing on messages and values to younger women, and women's needs in spirituality and prayer. Includes discussion guide.

Appendix A

Job Descriptions

Staff Liaison

Introduction

The Staff Liaison is a member of the church staff, who takes on the responsibility for introducing and developing the MOMS within the community. This person is the bridge between MOMS leaders and the church staff. The Staff Liaison is key in providing initial orientation, ongoing leadership training, and overall direction in adult spiritual formation.

Accountability

The Staff Liaison is accountable to the Director of Adult Education, Director of Family Ministry, Associate Pastor, or Church Council, as applicable in the community.

Responsibilities

1. Become aware of the theology, structure, content, and process of MOMS and how it fits in with your church community.
2. Recruit, train, supervise, and evaluate the team who works with the Coordinator for MOMS.
3. Propose a budget for MOMS and oversee its implementation.
4. Empower the Coordinator and her team in lay ministry by providing adequate office space or file cabinets, meeting space, support staff, and other resources as necessary.
5. Represent the MOMS at staff meetings, and represent the mission of the parish to the MOMS.
6. Prepare a yearly schedule for new MOMS groups (two to three per year) in coordination with other church programs and ministries.
7. Conduct evaluations and reports for the pastor and/or church council as needed.
8. Provide for ongoing participants of MOMS opportunities and resources for further education, faith development, and spiritual growth.
9. Be aware of professional resources within the community and make referrals as appropriate.

10. Develop a process in collaboration with other ministries whereby MOMS participants are encouraged and helped to share their talents within the community.

11. Purchase an adequate supply of *Called and Gifted* published by the United States Catholic Conference (Tel: 1-800-235-8722).

12. Become familiar with the theology and practical applications of *Called and Gifted*.

13. Prepare to help leaders and participants respond to their call to ministry, using *Called and Gifted* and a discernment process in Session 8.

14. Adapt the Continuing the Journey Worksheet (Appendix B) to fit the needs in your community.

Time Commitment

Approximately four hours a week in addition to other regular staff duties. Ten hours a week if the person is new on staff. The number of hours is related to the level of lay ministry training already available.

Qualifications:

- current staff member of church community
- thorough understanding of the adult educational process
- ability to reach out to new and alienated persons
- ability to train, affirm, and motivate lay leaders
- excellent communication and organizational skills

Benefits

- opportunity to draw women into a sense of fuller participation within the church community
- opportunity to lead families to further adult faith development through a non-threatening, welcoming structure
- opportunity to empower lay ministry in the church community

Coordinator of MOMS

Introduction

This person assists the staff in developing a team of lay ministers. She is the leader of the MOMS Core Team. This person listens to the needs of the lay ministers and helps provide the resources they need to serve MOMS in the church.

Accountability

The Coordinator of Ministry of Mothers Sharing is accountable to the Staff Liaison.

Responsibilities

To establish a communication schedule and evaluation process with ongoing training and affirmation for lay leaders. See Tasks below.

Time Commitment

Five hours per week, for one or two years.

Qualifications

- deep commitment to personal spiritual growth and a sense of the value of Christian community
- ability to communicate and organize materials and tasks
- ability to affirm lay leaders of varied skills and personalities
- ability to ask for and use pastoral supervision and consultation
- experience or degree in human services, communication, or pastoral ministry

Benefits

- opportunity to work with a variety of people
- develop and enhance leadership skills

- work with other Christian leaders
- become familiar with community resources

Tasks

1. Meet regularly with the Staff Liaison to plan the development of the MOMS in the community:
   a. Set annual goals and objectives.
   b. Establish budgets and record expenses.
   c. Prepare a schedule of MOMS events.

2. Recruit, affirm, and support volunteer leaders to establish and develop MOMS.

3. Develop orientation and schedule training for the team of Coordinators involved in the MOMS.

4. Schedule and set up office space and/or meeting space for the ministry.

5. Maintain program and ritual materials and supplies in a safe and orderly manner.

6. Meet monthly with Core Team to deal with issues and concerns that evolve as the ministry develops.
   a. Prepare agenda for meeting; record minutes.
   b. Report results to the Staff Liaison.
   c. Tabulate and review evaluations.
   d. Send communications of appreciation as needed.

7. Assist each team member clarify and process the situations that are causing frustration.

8. Follow through on tasks assigned by the Staff Liaison.

9. Keep accurate records of minutes and budget as needed.

10. Represent MOMS when requested.

Coordinator of Marketing & Publicity

Introduction

This person represents the church community and the Ministry of Mothers Sharing to potential participants. She is a member of the Core Team of MOMS. Through appropriate use of a variety of media, she raises awareness among the larger community of the benefits of MOMS. The Coordinator supervises a group of peers who plan, produce, and evaluate publicity.

Accountability

The Coordinator of Marketing is accountable to the Staff Liaison or the Coordinator of MOMS.

Responsibilities

To complete all the tasks listed below.

Time Commitment

One year, approximately two to four hours per week.

Qualifications

- familiarity with the structure and benefits of the MOMS
- familiarity with other church programs and ministries
- ability to handle a variety of phone calls and requests for information
- excellent communication skills and relationship skills
- ability to motivate, supervise, and affirm peers
- experience in marketing and/or ability to sell a product
- ability to handle criticism of MOMS or the church in a Christian, constructive manner

Benefits

- opportunity to put communication and marketing skills to use in a community environment

- opportunity to enhance leadership skills while strengthening community bonds

Tasks

Initial Preparations

1. Meet with the Staff Liaison for MOMS to present a one-year publicity plan for approval. The plan will include the following:

   a. A design for an informative flier and application for the initial six-week session. See Appendix B.

   b. A clear, specific series of bulletin announcements for the upcoming six-week session. (See sample in Appendix B.)

   c. A suggested series of pulpit announcements. (See Appendix B.)

   d. A plan for distributing publicity materials with specific dates and target population.

2. Recruit a publicity team who will do the following:

   a. Contact Leaders of the following groups: Baptism class, Childcare Ministry, Family Ministry, Religious Education at all age levels, Music and Liturgical Ministries, Church School, Administration, Church Secretaries and Receptionists, Women's Groups or Sodalities, etc.

   b. Provide information and printed materials to these groups so that they can promote MOMS on a regular basis.

   c. Be available at a table or booth after significant worship services, events or classes, to distribute publicity brochures.

   d. Make phone calls as necessary for recruitment.

Registration Process

1. Make phone calls to prospective participants. One personal call is more important than many fliers and letters.

2. Make your phone number available on publicity fliers for inquiries from parish leaders or prospective participants.

3. Keep a list of all inquiries with phone numbers for future reference. Note the nature of the inquiry and any reasons for not being able to attend (work on Tuesday evenings, for example). Note any changes needed in the publicity.

4. Establish a routine procedure (special folder, file, or computer listing) to follow up on names of potential future participants.

Immediate Preparations

Do the following at least two weeks before the first session:

1. Type in alphabetical order a list of participants' names, addresses, phone numbers.

2. Compile a list of names and ages of children for childcare ministry (if necessary).

3. Collect fees (if necessary) and application forms from each participant.

4. Prepare a financial record of all fees accepted and submit to Staff Liaison.

Ongoing Publicity

1. Develop a plan so that MOMS publicity becomes an integral part of all community information (e.g., parish ministry booklet, etc.).

2. Prepare publicity for any special events at the request of the Staff Liaison or the pastor.

3. Be available as a speaker for any community organization where the MOMS might be promoted.

Coordinator of Facilitators

Introduction

This person is a skilled facilitator who helps to develop these skills in teams of facilitators. Each team consists of three persons who create a safe learning environment: the Prayer Leader creates a sacred environment for prayer, the Guardian Angel creates an atmosphere of hospitality, and the Presenter facilitates the sharing of key concepts during each session.

Accountability

The Coordinator of Facilitators is accountable to the Staff Liaison and serves on the Core Team.

Responsibility

To complete the tasks listed below and report the results to the Core Team.

Time Commitment

Two years, approximately eight hours during the recruitment, training, and evaluation periods.

Qualifications

- knowledge of adult educational model
- ability to recruit, train, support, and evaluate other leaders
- understanding of the practical applications of U.S. Bishops' document *Called and Gifted*

Benefits

- opportunity to work with a variety of people and situations
- opportunity to enhance peer ministry skills in the community
- opportunity to be part of a training team
- opportunity to share and develop lay ministry

Tasks

1. Assists in training persons interested in peer ministry.
2. Recruits facilitator teams to provide the eight-week sessions.
3. Provides an orientation for each team and serves as a resource.
4. Conducts the Facilitator Team evaluation.
5. Reports to the Staff Liaison and the Core Team concerns, needs, and strengths of women in this leadership position.
6. Affirms facilitators at the Celebration of New Beginnings (Session 7).
7. Represents the needs of facilitators at Core Team planning.

Prayer Leader

Introduction

This person is responsible for creating a sacred environment for prayer, where the participants are welcomed and invited to express their ideas and feelings in various prayer rituals. She is a member of the Facilitator Team for MOMS.

Accountability

The Prayer Leader is accountable to the Coordinator of Facilitators.

Responsibilities

To prepare and conduct prayer rituals for one or more groups of MOMS in a six-month or year-long period. See tasks below.

Time Commitment

Three hours a week during the eight sessions plus time for Facilitator Team meetings (to be determined). One-year commitment preferable.

Qualifications

- ability to create an attractive prayer environment
- familiarity with prayer rituals
- sensitivity to a variety of prayer styles
- desire to develop skills in facilitating small groups
- ability to work well with others on a team

Benefits

- opportunity to lead a variety of prayer rituals
- opportunity to create a sacred time and place for community prayer
- increased sense of belonging in the community due to working on a team and ministering to others

Tasks

Pre-Session

1. Clarify with supervisor the budget available and the need to purchase prayer materials.
2. Prepare a storage place for ritual materials (see Preparation Checklist for Session 1).
3. Keep a financial record for purchases of any materials.
4. Read thoroughly the "Prayer Rituals" section of this book.
5. Meet weekly with the Facilitator Team for preparation and evaluation of each session.

For each session

1. Consult the prayer ritual section for the session, and practice doing the actual ritual so that directions and movements are clear and accurate.
2. Prepare the physical environment with prayer table, candle, and appropriate meditative music.
3. Prepare any special materials needed for the session (e.g., candles, butterflies, Serenity Prayer card, etc.).
4. Place ritual materials in storage after each session.

At the Celebration for New Beginnings:

1. Purchase one medium round loaf of bread and one pint of non-alcoholic wine.
2. Arrange for a Blessing Cup, napkin, and bread basket for the ritual.
3. Prepare prayer handouts for all attending.
4. Lead the opening and closing prayer rituals. See Prayer Ritual section.
5. Return all prayer ritual materials to storage.

Guardian Angel

Introduction

The Guardian Angel is in the key position to offer hospitality for the Ministry of Mothers Sharing. She is a member of the Facilitator Team. She creates a welcoming environment within which the participants are free to get to know each other, ask questions, and develop their sense of belonging.

Accountability

The Guardian Angel is accountable to the Coordinator of Facilitators.

Responsibilities

To assist in preparations and hospitality for one or more groups of MOMS participants during the year, and to maintain continual contact with participants during eight-week sessions. See below list of tasks and checklist on page 28 in Session Outlines.

Time Commitment

Four hours a week (two hours in session, two hours preparation), during the eight sessions. One-year commitment preferable.

Qualifications

- warm and welcoming personality
- ability to follow through on tasks
- good communication and organizational skills
- ability to participate in group process

Benefits

- opportunity to meet and welcome new people to the church community
- opportunity to develop and enhance leadership skills
- opportunity to grow spiritually and minister to others

Tasks

Pre-Session

1. Clarify with Coordinator of MOMS the budget available for refreshments, nametags, the *MOMS Journal*.

2. Prepare a storage place for materials.

3. Keep a financial record of purchases.

4. Obtain a list of participants from Coordinator of Marketing. Prepare a networking list containing all names, addresses, and telephone numbers for first session, for verification of all information.

5. Mail out a Letter of Welcome and What To Expect sheet to all participants ten to twelve days before first session. See Appendix B for examples.

6. Call participants and arrange for them to obtain a copy of *MOMS: A Personal Journal* at least one week before first session.

7. Prepare an eight-session sign-in sheet on a clipboard. Make nametags for the first session.

8. Set up hospitality table to welcome participants to the first session. On the table have the prepared nametags, pens, sign-in sheet, cash-box, and receipt book (if applicable).

9. Meet weekly with the Facilitator Team for preparation and evaluation of each session.

Each Session

1. Arrive approximately thirty minutes before each meeting.

2. Get room key from receptionist, if applicable.

3. Set up chairs in a circular arrangement around the prayer table.

4. Arrange for a board or large easel to be available in the room each week.

5. Recruit a volunteer from the group to help you set up the refreshment and hospitality tables each week.

6. Facilitate discussion of each week's topic by following the session outlines in this book.

7. Clean up the room after each session (with volunteers from among participants if possible) in accordance with the policy of your congregation or community.

8. Meet with the team of Facilitators for weekly 1½- to 2-hour planning sessions.

After First Session

1. A day or two after the first session, call each participant and ask:
    a. Do you have any questions about the experience?
    b. What was most helpful to you?
    c. What was most difficult for you?
    d. Have you called anyone from the group?

2. Alert the team to make clarifying announcements, if necessary.

General Tasks

1. Suggest that the group hold a Friendship Social at the home of one of the participants, to include spouses. (This will usually be held between second and third session. The person who hosts the event simply offers her home; other participants bring hors d'oeuvres and refreshments.) Guardian Angel arranges a simple icebreaker activity or game as a mixer.

2. Check if group would like to arrange:
    a. A mothers-and-children morning at a park.
    b. Other social activities between sessions.

3. When somebody misses a session, make a telephone call as soon as possible to pass on any announcements, to give an overview of that session's topic, and to alert them to next week's assignment.

4. Important: If somebody misses the first two sessions, call to suggest that she attend a later MOMS session that may not conflict with her schedule.

5. Prepare a file to contain all records: financial, attendance, evaluations.

Presenter

Introduction

The Presenter is the coordinator of the Facilitator Team. The Presenter has primary responsibility for all planning meetings each week, covering the key concepts, and timekeeping during the sessions.

Accountability

The Presenter is accountable to the Staff Liaison or Coordinator of Facilitators.

Responsibilities

To co-facilitate one or more eight-week sessions of MOMS during the year. To prepare for sessions and evaluate sessions in accordance with the Task listed below.

Time Commitment

Four hours a week (two hours preparation, two hours in session), during the eight sessions. Commitment of one year preferable.

Qualifications

- skills or willingness to be trained in group process and adult education learning models
- commitment to ongoing spiritual growth
- good communication and relationship skills
- ability to handle situations and others' personal problems with sensitivity
- ability to participate in a team decision-making process.
- ability to seek help when needed

Benefits

- chance to use group leadership skills in a small setting
- development of own spirituality while ministering to others

- opportunity to lead others to see more clearly their own giftedness
- opportunity to answer baptismal call to service in own church setting

Tasks

Pre-Session

1. Review this book so that all the content is familiar.
2. Read and complete *MOMS: A Personal Journal.*
3. Review the list of registered participants with the Staff Liaison to have a sense of the participants' ages, number of children, and goals for attending. If it appears that somebody is mistaking the group for a Scripture study, parenting class, or therapy group, make a clarifying call to that person.
4. Conduct the pre-session planning meeting.
5. Schedule dates for the eight planning meetings with the facilitators.

Each Session

1. Arrive fifteen to twenty minutes early to confirm any details or last-minute preparations with the team.
2. Welcome all participants as they arrive.
3. Conduct the session according to the Session Outlines.

After Each Session

1. Use Facilitator Reflection Page to do the following:
   a. Record your own ideas and feelings.
   b. Record your impressions of each person in the group, with a sensitivity to each person's need to participate. Note special gifts or skills of participants for use on Certificate of Achievement.
2. Plan the agenda for each team meeting.
3. At the team meeting, lead the team discussion on how to help each person participate more fully.
4. If there are any participants who have barriers that indicate they are uncomfortable participating and may be dealing with painful issues, call them to see if the team can do anything to make them more comfortable. If indicated, make them aware of the resources available to them in the church, in the local community, or through any suggested reading materials. Use Assessment Tool for referral to Staff Liaison, if necessary (see Appendix B).

After the Sixth Session

1. Review and tabulate the participants' evaluations with the team.

2. Make recommendations to the Staff Liaison or MOMS Coordinator for improvements.

3. Confirm the date, time, and place of the Facilitator Evaluation with the Staff Liaison and other team members.

Coordinator of Childcare

Introduction

Quality childcare is an absolute necessity for the ministry to be a success. The Coordinator of Childcare establishes consistent, quality childcare during each MOMS session. She is a member of the MOMS Core Team and the chief liaison between the childcare providers and the parents.

Accountability

The Coordinator of Childcare is accountable to the Staff Liaison or Coordinator of MOMS, as applicable.

Responsibilities

The Childcare Coordinator will attend Core Team planning and evaluation meetings as necessary. She will also need to recruit, train, and evaluate childcare providers for each MOMS session and the Celebration of New Beginnings. She must establish clear routine procedures for the childcare ministry and provide a safe, stimulating environment for the children in care. Finally, she is to carry out all tasks required for consistent, quality childcare (see Tasks below).

Time Commitment

Four hours per week (six to ten hours per week if this is the first time childcare is offered.) Commitment of one year preferable.

Qualifications

- ability to motivate others
- organization and communication skills
- experience working in settings related to children (e.g., schools, preschools, childcare, etc.)
- ability to work with childcare providers of varied skills, ages, and personalities
- ability to enforce rules and local regulations concerning health and safety
- ability to work tactfully with parents

Coordinator of Childcare

Benefits

- opportunity to learn to work with a variety of people
- opportunity to develop and enhance leadership skills
- opportunity to express commitment to lay ministry
- opportunity to facilitate the development of a ministry by providing an essential service to participants

Tasks

Four Weeks Ahead

1. Prepare a budget for childcare and submit to Staff Liaison or Coordinator of MOMS for approval.
2. Recruit volunteer childcare providers (babysitters) for the upcoming eight sessions.
3. Type a list of childcare volunteers' names, addresses, phone numbers, for your own use.
4. Reserve one or more rooms suitable for children, either at the facility where the MOMS group meets or at a nearby location.
5. Prepare typed list of guidelines, policies, and procedures for those using the childcare room, to have available for parents and volunteer childcare providers.

Two to Three Weeks Ahead

1. Obtain a list of children registered for childcare from the MOMS Coordinator or Coordinator of Marketing. Verify that you have an appropriate ratio of adults to children. (Suggested ratio is minimum five to one preschoolers to adults, with a two to one ratio necessary for infants).
2. Prepare sign-in sheets, snack sign-up sheets, welcome letter, nametags, and simple craft activities. (It may be easier to delegate crafts to one of the volunteers.)
3. Prepare a list of children and assign each volunteer to an age group or specific children.

One Week Ahead

1. Schedule an orientation meeting with volunteer childcare providers approximately one week before the MOMS training/orientation session begins. At that meeting, clearly outline their duties (craft activities, reading, singing, cleanup duties). Have their responsibilities typed on a list as a help to them.

MOMS: Developing A Ministry APPENDIX A:
Job Descriptions

2. Establish the discipline techniques childcare providers are expected to use.

3. Assign to one childcare provider the responsibility of welcoming parents and sign-in/out procedures.

4. If parents pay a fee for childcare, designate the person responsible for accepting all payments.

During Sessions

1. Check that the rooms used are well-lit, childproof, and clean (toys, tables, cribsheets).

2. Verify that all childcare providers arrive as scheduled. (If somebody is absent, call them as soon as possible to find out what emergency prevented their arrival.)

3. Check that art supplies, snacks, refreshments, are adequate.

4. Obtain a weekly update from the childcare providers and address any concerns or difficult issues.

5. Keep accurate financial records if parents are paying a fee for childcare.

6. Ensure that cleanup procedures and lockup of the facilities are properly carried out.

After Last Session

1. Ask childcare providers for feedback on the eight-week experience (what went well, improvements needed, etc.). Make an evaluation report for your records and submit one to the MOMS Coordinator. Include recommendations for church leaders, if applicable.

2. Write a thank-you letter to each childcare provider.

3. Keep a list of childcare providers who expressed willingness to commit to another eight weeks at a later date.

Coordinator,
Celebration of New Beginnings

Introduction

The Coordinator of this Celebration is a member of the Core Team of MOMS. This person is responsible for coordinating the tasks needed to provide the celebration dinner for Session 7. This event includes social, spiritual, and intellectual affirmation for the women of MOMS. The event may be attended by pastoral staff as well as past participants of the MOMS. The Coordinator supervises a group of peers who plan, provide, and evaluate this community event. This team of peers may be asked to provided the luncheon for training in peer ministry.

Accountability

The Coordinator of the Celebration of New Beginnings is accountable to the Staff Liaison or Coordinator of MOMS, as applicable.

Responsibilities

To plan and oversee one or more Celebrations of New Beginnings per year in accordance with the Tasks below.

Time Commitment

Two hours a week during the six weeks prior to each Celebration. One year commitment to the Team.

Qualifications

- belief in celebrations and Christian community
- ability to motivate, supervise, and affirm peers
- ability to clearly define and delegate tasks
- good communication and organizational skills
- healthy self-esteem and sense of humor

MOMS: Developing A Ministry

Benefits

- sense of accomplishment in coordinating an important community-building experience for MOMS participants and staff
- enhancement of leadership skills put into practice over a limited time

Tasks

Pre-Event Preparations

1. Read "Session 7: Celebration of New Beginnings," beginning on page 70, thoroughly. Read also pages 95–96.
2. Schedule a date, location (church facility or restaurant), menu, and speaker.
3. Confirm speaker and stipend (needs staff approval in writing).
4. Clarify budget limitations with the Staff Liaison, accept RSVP payments and compile a complete financial report.
5. Maintain a mailing list and address labels of past participants and staff to be invited.
6. Select a dining-room hostess for the event.
7. Prepare an agenda for the event. See sample agenda on page 73.

Pre-Event Preparations for Celebration Team

1. Design and reproduce an invitation with a MOMS logo and RSVP process. Distribute invitations (see Appendix B) to participants, guests, and staff after the third session.
2. Prepare a dining-room floor plan, seating arrangements, and decor (table decorations, lighting, favors). Arrange for a hospitality table and gathering rite (food or icebreaker activity).
3. Recruit an MC. Establish a schedule for the evening. Arrange for appropriate expressions of appreciation (words or gifts). Organize cleanup crew.
4. Arrange for an appropriate opening and closing prayer ritual. Consider asking the Prayer Leader from the team.

Event and Follow-up

1. Oversee the team as they carry out the tasks for the celebration.

MOMS: Developing A Ministry
APPENDIX A:
Job Descriptions

2. Compile an evaluation of the celebration. See Appendix B. Hand this out to four or five selected persons at the celebration. Use feedback from these for future planning.

3. Write thank-you notes to the speaker and those who donated time, talent, and/or money. Remember to include the Celebration Team in your "thank you's."

4. Attend the monthly core team meetings. Share a summary of the Celebration evaluations and a financial report.

5. Coordinate other celebrations as determined by the Core Team.

6. Provide the meals for peer ministry training when needed.

Coordinator of Prayer Ministry/Retreats

Introduction

This person assists the community and the Core Team of MOMS by developing a community of women who are praying for the spiritual success of the ministry as part of the community. She may be asked to help initiate mornings or evenings of prayer or a MOMS retreat.

Accountability

The Coordinator of Prayer Ministry/Retreats is accountable to the Coordinator of MOMS.

Responsibility

To complete the tasks listed below.

Time Commitment

One year, approximately eight hours during recruitment and two hours each during the weeks of Sessions 5 and 7. More if asked to do retreats.

Qualifications

- belief in the power of persons praying for each other
- ability to reach out and motivate and affirm other women

Benefits

- opportunity to reach out to and communicate with a large network of persons of all ages
- opportunity to establish community times of prayer and specific retreat experiences
- opportunity to raise awareness of the value of prayer

Tasks

1. Recruit by phone a prayer sponsor for each person attending MOMS (organize a list of names, addresses, and phone numbers for mailings).

2. Mail each prayer sponsor the letter with suggested activities for the eight weeks (see from letter, Appendix B).

3. Collect and present the small gifts at Session 5 (prepare one or two small gifts in case someone does not show up).

4. Give the Coordinator of the Celebration of New Beginnings a list on names, addresses, and phone numbers to invite to Session 7.

5. Keep an accurate list of names of persons contacted for this ministry so that someone who does not want to be contacted is not recontacted by a new person.

6. Attend and encourage all prayer sponsors to attend Session 7: Celebration of New Beginnings. Purchase small appreciation gifts for prayer sponsors. Introduce prayer sponsors and thank them for their significant contribution to the spiritual growth of the Christian community.

7. Have a liturgy or prayer service at the end of the year for all persons who have been part of this ministry.

8. Possibly coordinate morning or evening prayer or a MOMS retreat for all mothers in the community.

Coordinator of Resources

Introduction

This person is a member of the Core Team of MOMS. She is key in synthesizing the concerns and talents of all the groups, especially those of new participants. She provides resources for continued spiritual development for ongoing groups.

Accountability

The Coordinator of Resources is accountable to the Staff Liaison or Coordinator of MOMS, as applicable.

Responsibilities

To provide educational resources and information on the community to MOMS participants after the Celebration. Assists in integration of participants into lay ministry in accordance with their gifts and the needs of the community. See tasks below.

Time Commitment

Two hours per week, for one year.

Qualifications

- commitment to ongoing spiritual growth
- good planning and organizational skills
- ability to represent the Christian community
- ability to network people and resources

Benefits

- chance to become familiar with community resources
- opportunity to bring speakers, programs, and other resources the community
- opportunity to develop personal spirituality while ministering to others

Tasks

1. Read the Resources section beginning on page 105 of this book. Order and preview materials published for small groups, spiritual growth and group development.

2. Develop a library of books and videos and make available as study materials for ongoing groups.

3. For Session 8 (Discernment: Continuing the Journey), assist Staff Liaison in making participants aware of ongoing opportunities for growth. Give dates of spirituality, catechetical or parenting classes; give contact names and numbers for Ministry Coordinators within the community (e.g., Christian Initiation, Social Justice Outreach, Family Ministry, Divorce/Separation Outreach, etc.).

4. Review the completed "Time and Talent" form and the evaluations to see the special gifts of the participants. Invite participants with special skills to be involved in ministry within the church community.

5. After Session 8, conduct a session with each ongoing group to orient participants to videos, publications and other resources available at the church or in community libraries. Provide website and e-mail addresses of people who are willing to share their ideas for successful ongoing groups.

6. Appoint a contact person in each ongoing group; coordinate a calendar of monthly or biweekly meetings for each group; maintain regular communication with the contact person of each group, reminding groups to never become isolationist and to avoid becoming exclusive; encourage community outreach ventures as a valuable component of any small faith community; facilitate twice-yearly self-evaluations with each group to discern ongoing growth directions.

7. Schedule a yearly networking day or day of renewal for ongoing MOMS groups (in collaboration with the Coordinator of Prayer Ministry/Retreats). Invite a local retreat director or spiritual director to lead the event.

8. Evaluate each event for new ideas and improvements. Prepare an annual report of all activities and submit to the Core Team and Staff Liaison.

Coordinator of Peer Ministry Training

Introduction

This person assists the Staff Liaison in the development of lay ministry in the parish for MOMS by organizing the recruitment, publicity, and evaluation of leadership training in peer ministry.

Accountability

The Coordinator of Peer Ministry Training is accountable to the Staff Liaison or the Coordinator of MOMS, as applicable.

Responsibilities

To complete the tasks listed below and report the results to the Core Team.

Time Commitment

One year, approximately eight hours a week during recruitment (two months) and two hours a week during training and evaluation (two months).

Qualifications

- familiarity with lay ministry training
- involvement in ongoing spiritual formation
- ability to handle a variety of phone calls
- ability to motivate, coordinate, and affirm peers

Benefits

- opportunity to develop and use training and workshop skills
- opportunity to work on teamwork skills in lay ministry
- opportunity to work with a wide variety of people, situations, and skills

Tasks

1. Confirm dates and space for the Leadership in Peer Ministry training session with the Staff Liaison after the planning meeting.

2. With the Coordinator of MOMS, circulate the publicity and registration materials prepared by the Staff Liaison.

3. Personally call and invite the MOMS "graduates" to consider attending this training for their continued spiritual development. (Keep a list of those who are/are not interested.)

4. Prepare manuals and workshop materials (e.g., name tags, attendance sheet).

5. Confirm luncheon plans with Coordinator of Celebration of New Beginnings.

6. Mobilize the Core Team as necessary to help with this area of ministry.

Appendix B

Forms

Announcement Flier

To use the announcement flier on opposite page "as is," white out the designated places and fill in with your own information. If your copy machine does double-sided copies, photocopy back to back with Registration Form on reverse.

Mary shared her feelings with Elizabeth.

"How much it meant to share the faith, the fear, the anticipation with a trusted friend" ...
— THE VISITATION

MINISTRY OF MOTHERS SHARING

An opportunity for women to develop self-esteem, relationship skills, and a more defined sense of their own spirituality at a time when they are facing the difficult challenges of raising a family.

MINISTRY OF MOTHERS SHARING will be led by a team of facilitators and topics will include . . .

1. **Self-Esteem & Self-Acceptance**
   What influences me at this time in my life?

2. **Stress, Worries, and Anxiety**
   Learning to deal with stress productively.

3. **Everyday Spirituality**
   Relationship with self, relationship with God.

4. **Feelings**
   Constructive self-expression.

5. **Personal Growth**
   Who am I? Where do I give and receive support?

6. **Expressing Values in Friendships**
   Defining Christian values, examining relationships.

7. **Celebration of New Beginnings**
   An evening of celebration.

8. **Discernment: Continuing the Journey**
   How will I continue my personal growth? How am I "called" to continue my personal growth?

Cost is *(insert your cost here)* and includes one copy of the book **MOMS: A Personal Journal** by Paula Hagen & Vickie LoPiccolo Jennett.

Make checks payable to:

   (Insert name of community here)

CHILDCARE will be available at no extra charge, but you must reserve a place for your child (see over).

Upon registration you may pick up your reading materials. Bring completed registration and payment to:

   (Insert community name & address here)

Questions? Call: *(Insert community phone number here.)*

M.O.M.S.

WHO:

WOMEN who devote their time to the spiritual and physical upbringing of their children.

WOMEN who live stressful lives.

WOMEN who live with many demands on their time and energy.

WOMEN who need a place to receive personal and spiritual nurturing.

WHAT:

Learn to share with mothers of all ages the stress, concerns and positive experiences that have influenced your personal growth.

Experience the support of other women as you discover the depth of your spirituality.

WHEN:

(Insert dates & times here)

All groups run 8 weeks, which includes a celebration dinner (Session 7), a discussion of *Called and Gifted*, and a discernment of how you are "called" to proceed on the journey.

WHERE:

(Insert location here)

REQUIREMENTS:

The ability to make a commitment to an initial 8-week period. The ability to keep confidentiality. A desire to grow by sharing. The ability to support other mothers in their personal growth.

Ministry of Mothers Sharing (MOMS) Registration Form

Date_____

Name _____
         Last   First   Middle

Address _____
        Number & Street   City   State

Phone (Home)_____ (Work)_____ Age _____

Employer _____

Full Time Homemaker? Yes No

Children (names and ages) _____

_____

_____

Level of Education (Check One)
- ☐ Grade School ☐ High School
- ☐ College ☐ Advanced Degree(s):_____

Registered at this church? Yes No

How long have you lived in this community? _____

Do you have family here? Yes No

Have you ever joined any other support group? Yes No

If yes, name group and state the benefits received_____

_____

Why are you interested in this group? (Check those that apply.)

- ☐ Intellectual ☐ Spiritual ☐ Psychological/Emotional
- ☐ Social ☐ Other (Please be specific)_____

What personal talents or skills do you bring to this group? (e.g., music, crafts, good listener)

_____

What are your expectations about this group?_____

_____

What do you need from the persons in leadership?_____

_____

Will your child need care during the sessions? Yes No

Name_____Age _____Special Needs _____

Name_____Age _____Special Needs _____

Name_____Age _____Special Needs _____

Office Use Only:
Date received_____ **Amount** _____ **Paid** _____ **Scholarship**_____

MOMS: Developing A Ministry
© 2001 Resource Publications, Inc. All rights reserved.

Sample Pulpit Announcements

Introducing MOMS As a New Ministry

"Good morning. I am Sarah White. I have lived in this parish for two years and have two children aged 3 and 7.

"I am here to inform you about a special new ministry we are establishing here at St. Paul's. MOMS means Ministry of Mothers Sharing.

"As you may have seen in last week's bulletin (or flier), it is an 8-week program where mothers come together to share readings from this book (hold up *Journal*), pray, and discuss issues affecting our lives. For me, there are three exciting things about MOMS:

1. I will have a chance to talk with other mothers about the stress of being a mother.

2. I will learn how to plan time for myself as I minister to my family.

3. I will discover how being a mother really is a ministry.

"With (name of Staff Liaison), we have established a core team of mothers who will begin the first session Thursday, September 10, from 7 to 9 P.M. I am here today to invite you to register after Mass (or the service) for one of these sessions. We need to have you register today so that the participants can pick up their books (hold up *Journal*) and prepare for the first session Thursday, September 10.

"Childcare is available for those who register their children.

"Please pray that this ministry will blossom and strengthen our whole parish or community. For more information, see the flier insert in the bulletin, or stop by the registration table on your way out."

Promoting MOMS As an Existing Ministry

"(Greeting as above.)

"I would like to take a few minutes to speak about MOMS, Ministry of Mothers Sharing, here at St. James. You have probably seen the fliers and announcements in the bulletin (or at the back of the church).

"When I became a new mother six years ago, I put my spirituality on hold, more or less. I had no one to share that part of my life with.

"MOMS offered me the opportunity to meet for discussion, support and prayer with other women who were in a situation similar to mine. I discovered a relaxed, comfortable place where I could just be myself, learn about myself, and grow spiritually. The women in the group supported me, and I found I had a lot to offer them, too.

"MOMS has helped me to belong to St. James' community in a *real* way."

(Continue, giving specific details as in previous example.)

Sample Bulletin Announcement

To use the bulletin announcement on opposite page "as is," white out the designated places and fill in with your own information.

Christ the King

CATHOLIC COMMUNITY NEWSLETTER

1551 E. Dana Ave. • Mesa, Arizona 85204 • (602) 964-1719

Ministry of Mothers Sharing
"MOMS"
Tuesday mornings, 9:00 am–11:00 am
Eight weeks, beginning January 14, 1991

"It means so much to be able to talk to other mothers who understand."

Bring the companionship of other women into your busy life as a mother! Enjoy this opportunity to develop your self-esteem and enhance your relationship skills in the company of other mothers. Take a few hours each week to develop a greater awareness of your own spirituality as a mother, and to appreciate the ministry of your motherhood!

"I find being a mother so much easier since MOMS."

MOMS has welcomed more than 75 women at Christ the King and has active groups in 15–20 parishes in Arizona. Don't miss this opportunity to do something special for yourself. Register THIS WEEK by filling out the form on the reverse of the MOMS brochure and dropping it into the Family Ministry Office. Cost is $30.00. Partial scholarships are available.

"I come to church on Sunday now and I recognize people from MOMS. It has given me a real feeling of belonging."

Sample Letter of Welcome

(room for letterhead)

(Date)

Dear   ,

We were pleased to receive your registration for the Ministry of Mothers Sharing. The group will meet from 7 to 9 p.m. on Thursday evenings for eight weeks beginning February 1 and continuing through March 15. Sessions will be held in the Living room in the Cullen building. There will be a special celebration the evening of *(date)* at *(time)* P.M. in Cullen Hall.

It is essential that we start and end promptly. Please check in fifteen minutes before the session begins, so you can meet the other mothers.

If you will be placing a child in the childcare room, please allow some extra time for check-in. Be sure to label all your child's belongings. If your child is apprehensive, make a cheerful, but firm goodbye, at a brisk pace. The childcare providers will contact you if your child needs you during the session.

This experience will be conducted by a team of facilitators. They share willingly of their time, as they facilitate the process of forming this new spiritual support group.

You received your copy of *MOMS: A Personal Journal* when you registered. Please take time to read and reflect on the first session, "Self-Esteem and Self-Acceptance," before our first meeting on *(date)*. Reading each chapter and doing the activities is important to get the full benefit from the MOMS.

Congratulations on taking the time to do something special for yourself. As a woman and a mother, you are the one person who knows what you need in your life. As you know, this is not a Bible study group, counseling group, or parenting class. It is designed for your spiritual growth.

Enclosed please find a copy of "What to Expect in Ministry of Mothers Sharing." If you have any questions or concerns, please contact *(name)* at *(phone number)*. Remember to bring *MOMS: A Personal Journal* to class with you. You will need your answers to participate in the discussion.

Sincerely,

Staff Liaison

Coordinator of MOMS

What to Expect in Ministry of Mothers Sharing (MOMS)

This group is for you. As you prepare for the upcoming sessions, please note the following so that you can gain the most from the experience:

- **Opportunity for Growth.** This group will meet for eight weeks. In the seventh week, we will have a Celebration of New Beginnings. After the Celebration, you will have a chance to choose new opportunities for growth for yourself and your family.

- **Punctuality.** The group will begin and end promptly because of childcare. Please be on time to respect our time limitations.

- **Adult Learning Model.** As adults, you have a wealth of experience and knowledge to bring to the learning adventure. Therefore, the group will often break into small groups of two or three to facilitate the sharing of ideas. Your thoughts and opinions are valued and will not be judged.

- **Experiential Learning.** Reflective questions have been designed to give you some new experiences of spiritual growth and relationships. Read the text of *MOMS: A Personal Journal* and complete all journaling exercises before coming to each session. You are never asked to show your journal to anyone. Having your thoughts written down will make them easier to share.

- **Holistic Spirituality.** The experience will include exercises to nurture the sacred within you. Many women experience an inner awakening, a renewed energy, or a desire to continue to meet and discuss other issues.

- **Prayer.** A variety of prayer forms and rituals, including both traditional and contemporary prayers, will broaden your experience of prayer. Inclusive language is used. A person in our church community has agreed to be your "prayer sponsor" for these eight sessions. She will be praying for you and will be invited to the seventh session.

- **Confidentiality.** The things we learn about each other in the sessions must remain within the group. This is essential if we are to build a system of trust.

- **Evaluation.** Each person's evaluation of this experience is valuable. Completing the evaluation will help indicate a direction for you and for MOMS. An evaluation form will be given out at the fifth session.

- **Family Perspective.** You will be invited to a Friendship Social so you and your husband or friend can meet the husbands/ friends of the other women. A Family Perspective session will be made available as an option after the eighth session.

Sample Letter to Prayer Sponsor

Dear Friend in Ministry:

Thank you for saying yes to my phone call asking you to be a prayer sponsor for one of the ten women who are attending the current MOMS group. The sessions will begin on (*date*) and continue until (*date*). We are asking you to reach out with daily prayer and a weekly reach-out activity.

The person for whom you will be praying is: _____

Her address is: _____

Her phone number is: _____

Suggested Activities:

Week 1	Pray for your person and her family.
Week 2	Call her and tell her you are her prayer sponsor.
Week 3	Mail her a small card.
Week 4	Call and see how the MOMS group is going for her.
Week 5	Prepare a plant, flowers, cookies, or other small item, which the Facilitator Team will present to her on (*date of Session 5*). Please drop off your small gift at (*location*) before (*date and time*), or contact me at (*phone number*).
Week 6	Write an encouraging note.
Week 7	Attend the Celebration of New Beginnings on (*date*). You will receive an invitation.
Week 8	Stay in touch with your person any way you choose.

We thank you for your very important spiritual support for these women who are seeking to grow closer to God.

Looking forward to seeing you on (*date of Celebration dinner*).

Sincerely in Christ,

Coordinator of Prayer Ministry

Staff Liaison

MOMS: Developing A Ministry

Certificate of Achievement Preparation Form

To Facilitator Team: After each session, record special gifts or talents you notice in each participant. This will help you prepare the Certificates of Achievement to be given out in Session 7. It will also help the team focus on the gifts of each person.

1. NAME & PHONE NUMBER: _____

_____

_____

_____

_____

2. NAME & PHONE NUMBER: _____

_____

_____

_____

_____

3. NAME & PHONE NUMBER: _____

_____

_____

_____

_____

4. NAME & PHONE NUMBER: _____

_____

_____

_____

_____

5. NAME & PHONE NUMBER: _____

_____

_____

_____

_____

6. NAME & PHONE NUMBER:_____

_____

_____

_____

_____

7. NAME & PHONE NUMBER:_____

_____

_____

_____

_____

8. NAME & PHONE NUMBER:_____

_____

_____

_____

_____

9. NAME & PHONE NUMBER:_____

_____

_____

_____

_____

10. NAME & PHONE NUMBER:_____

_____

_____

_____

_____

Assessment Tool for Referral to Staff Liaison

Facilitator Team: Occasionally, a participant shows concrete signs of needing services or support that are beyond the scope of MOMS. Use this form as a checklist if you feel a participant is showing certain signs that indicate a need for professional help. Complete form and submit to Staff Liaison. Do not attempt to make a referral yourself.

Participant's Name _____ Phone _____

Physical Signs

☐ Often comes late, looking hassled and exhausted.
☐ Seems nervous, anxious, and tense.
☐ Often cries or seems on the verge of tears.
☐ Appears grief-stricken about a recent trauma in the family.
☐ Appears very fatigued.

Social/Emotional Signs

☐ Always passes when invited to participate.
☐ Asks an inappropriate number of questions at each session.
☐ Appears isolated with no social or personal contacts.
☐ Seems to have a lot of inner conflict or unresolved personal issues.

Verbal Signs

☐ Talks about a lot of childhood abuse or violence.
☐ Talks about violence in her marriage or family relationships.
☐ Uses language that might indicate long-term anger or resentment.
☐ Talks excessively about problems.
☐ Often complains of depression.
☐ Speaks very negatively about her family and herself.
☐ Reveals that she is afraid of abusing her children.*
☐ Other _____

* **Important:** Any knowledge of child abuse must by law be reported to authorities. Refer to Staff Liaison immediately.

Submitted by _____

Date_____

For staff use only:
Follow-up phone call made _____
Appointment made for_____
Action taken_____

Referred to _____

MOMS Participant's Evaluation Form

This evaluation of your learning experience is important to us. It will also help us improve the experience for other participants in the future. Please return this at the end of the eighth session.

Rate each aspect of the eight-week experience:

Small group sharing	Very Helpful	1	2	3	4	5	Not Helpful
Mini-presentations	Very Helpful	1	2	3	4	5	Not helpful
MOMS Journal book	Very Helpful	1	2	3	4	5	Not Helpful
Prayer Rituals	Very Helpful	1	2	3	4	5	Not Helpful
Networking List	Very Helpful	1	2	3	4	5	Not Helpful
Friendship Social	Very Helpful	1	2	3	4	5	Not Helpful

Rate the value of each individual session:

Session 1: Self-Esteem...	Very Helpful	1	2	3	4	5	Not Helpful
Session 2: Stress...	Very Helpful	1	2	3	4	5	Not Helpful
Session 3: Everyday Spirituality	Very Helpful	1	2	3	4	5	Not Helpful
Session 4: Feelings	Very Helpful	1	2	3	4	5	Not Helpful
Session 5: Personal Growth	Very Helpful	1	2	3	4	5	Not Helpful
Session 6: Expressing Values	Very Helpful	1	2	3	4	5	Not Helpful
Session 7: Celebration of New...	Very Helpful	1	2	3	4	5	Not Helpful
Session 8: Discernment:...	Very Helpful	1	2	3	4	5	Not Helpful

The most helpful aspect for me personally was _____

_____

The least helpful aspect for me personally was _____

_____

I would improve this experience by _____

_____

Did this experience impact on your couple relationship? How? _____

_____

_____

_____

Did this experience impact on your family relationships? How? _____

_____

_____

_____

Please use reverse for additional comments.

Name_____Phone _____Date _____

　　　　　Forms

Celebration of New Beginnings Evaluation Form

In order to plan and provide activities that serve the needs of MOMS, we need to evaluate our events. You have been picked to evaluate this celebration. Your time, ideas, and suggestions are appreciated and will be respected. Your name will remain confidential. Please use the reverse side if you need more space. Please be specific. That is most helpful.

Environment:

Was the place, schedule, and atmosphere conducive to celebration? _____

_____

Hospitality:

Was everyone welcomed, introduced to other guests, and helped to feel welcome? _____

_____

Celebration Meal:

Did the table arrangements promote conversation and community between all MOMS participants, past participants, and guests? _____

_____

Prayer Rituals and Speaker:

Did these facilitate personal involvement and building of community? _____

_____

Other Comments (use reverse if needed): _____

_____

_____

_____

_____

_____

_____

Enclosed please find a stamped self-addressed envelope. Please return it to the Staff Liaison immediately for our report. Thank you for your ministry.

Name_____Phone_____Date_____

Facilitator Team Evaluation Form

As a member of the Facilitator Team, you have the opportunity to offer valuable feedback that will help to improve the MOMS and adapt it to the needs of this community. The participants have evaluated their experience, and now the staff needs your insights. Please be specific as you answer the questions below.

MOMS Sessions

Hospitality:

Was everyone introduced to each other and helped to feel welcome? Yes No

Comments: _____

_____

Environment:

Were the room, schedule, and table arrangements helpful to the group process? Yes No

Comments: _____

_____

Topics:

Were you able to keep the group on topic within the time limitations? Yes No

Comments: _____

_____

MOMS Journal:

Were you able to facilitate each participant's sharing of her experiences and insights? Yes No

_____

Comments: _____

_____

Prayer Rituals:

Did the prayer rituals fit the needs of the participants and the goals of the session? Yes No

In what way? _____

_____

Adult Learning:

What was the most valuable thing that you learned from this experience? I learned _____

_____

_____

Name the leadership skills that you strengthened: _____

_____

Please continue on reverse.

Personal Satisfaction in Ministry

What motivated you to serve in this ministry?_____

_____

Did you fulfill your personal goals for volunteering your time and talents? Yes No

Please explain your answer: _____

_____

Did being on the MOMS Facilitator Team strengthen your own spiritual growth? Yes No

Please explain your answer: _____

_____

Did being on the MOMS Facilitator Team strengthen your own marriage? Yes No

Please explain your answer: _____

_____

Did being on the MOMS Facilitator Team strengthen your family life? Yes No

If you could change one thing in your job description or performance on the team, what would you change? _____

_____

How many hours did you volunteer in order to complete the tasks of your job description?

Before _____ **After**_____ **During the six weeks** _____

Who or what was the most supportive to you? _____

_____

In what way would you like to continue to be involved in MOMS? _____

_____

Who in the group do you recommend for facilitator training or involvement in the ministry?_____

_____

Additional Comments: _____

_____

_____

_____

_____

_____

_____

_____

Name_____Phone _____Date _____

MOMS: Developing A Ministry

Time and Talent Form

Background Information

Name _____ Phone _____

Address _____

Level of Education (Check One)
- ☐ Grade School
- ☐ College
- ☐ High School
- ☐ Advanced Degree(s) _____

Occupation _____

Employer _____

Check One:
- ☐ Single
- ☐ Separated
- ☐ Married
- ☐ Divorced

Children's Names and Ages _____

_____

_____

_____

_____

Volunteer and/or Leadership Experience

Note any volunteer or paid leadership experience with church or civic organizations (Marriage Encounter, Cursillo, Hospital Volunteer, Scout Leader, etc.):

Number of Years	**Description of Position**
_____	Years of married life
_____	Years of parenting (Parents are leaders.)
_____	_____
_____	_____
_____	_____
_____	_____
_____	_____

Please continue on reverse.

Worksheet — Called & Gifted

Past leaders composed this list of skills. No one person has developed all these skills. The Holy Spirit gives different gifts for a variety of tasks. The purpose of this list is not to intimidate, but to raise awareness of skills you may already have and need to develop in the leadership position. Trust the Holy Spirit, who guides and strengthens us to do God's work.

Please rate yourself on a scale of 1 to 5 (1 = low and 5 = high). Then go back, star (*) your two greatest strengths, and double star (**) your two greatest weaknesses as a leader.

_____ Ability to keep confidentiality.

_____ Ability to say "no" to things not in the job description (stay focused).

_____ Ability to state ideas clearly.

_____ Ability to give clear instructions.

_____ Ability to support other leaders.

_____ Ability to listen and affirm others.

_____ Ability to give and receive constructive criticism (honest feedback).

_____ Ability to support staff (persons in authority) and to refer others in need to them.

_____ Ability not to internalize negative comments (personalize).

_____ Ability to attend meetings on a regular basis.

_____ Ability to complete tasks alone.

_____ Ability to complete tasks with others.

_____ Ability to motivate others.

_____ Ability to clearly organize and delegate tasks.

_____ Ability to manage time well.

_____ Ability to work in a large group or team.

_____ Ability to work with other leaders on a goal or project.

_____ Ability to lead and conduct meetings using an agenda.

_____ Ability to work in a close relationship with a variety of people.

_____ Ability to make decisions and facilitate the group making decisions.

_____ Ability to oversee planning of major events.

_____ Ability to meet deadlines.

_____ Ability to write letters.

_____ Ability to speak clearly in a large group.

Personal Discernment Worksheet

The realities of adult and family life challenge me to change and develop my spirituality. This challenge draws me closer to God's love for me and encourages me to use my gifts. This process is one of discernment. Discernment, like decision-making, is not easy nor comfortable, but it is an essential skill for Christian living.

What is discernment? Discernment is the awareness of the Spirit's presence and guidance in the decisions of my life. Discernment calls me to remain open to all the possibilities God may be offering me. Discernment happens through the concrete: through knowing myself, trusting in God, and being open to the suggestions of friends and mentors.

Now, I must discern. What have I learned about myself in this MOMS group? What do I need to do now for my own spiritual and mental well-being? What decisions must I make now so that the peace-filled Spirit of God shows through me? With whom must I discuss these questions so that true discernment happens?

After prayerful consideration and discussion with those who will support me and be affected by this decision (my family or friends), I have determined the following as areas in which I most desire growth:

In my personal development, I choose to focus on _____
_____
_____
_____

In my family, I choose to pay attention to _____
_____
_____
_____

In my friendships, I choose to pay attention to _____
_____
_____
_____

How do these commitments support my relationship with God? _____
_____
_____

In order to balance in-home and away-from-home activities, I will concentrate on _____
_____
_____

After spending time in prayer and decision-making, complete the "Continuing the Journey" worksheet in preparation for Session 8.

Continuing the Journey Worksheet

Adapt the following for your own community.

Listed here are some of the options for continued opportunities for spiritual growth in our community. Please check only the ones you can do. This worksheet will be referred to in Session 8.

I. Involvement in Ministry

❑ I am already committed to the ministry of_____

❑ I am involved in the Council of Catholic Women in the area of _____

❑ I hope to be trained in leadership in peer ministry. (See flier with application.)

❑ I hope to become involved in (check all that apply):

❑ MOMS	❑ communion ministry	❑ bereavement
❑ Wee Worship	❑ lectoring at Mass	❑ children's liturgy
❑ youth ministry	❑ the community school	❑ ministry to sick and elderly
❑ Other		

II. Plans for the Future

I would like to continue to meet as a MOMS group. Yes No

Frequency of meetings:

❑ once a week	❑ every other week	❑ monthly

Topics I would like to discuss further:

❑ family traditions	❑ women and spirituality	❑ communication
❑ prayer	❑ Other(s)_____	

Date and Time of next meeting_____

Place _____

Facilitator _____

Vatican Council II Fact Sheet:
Called and Gifted for the Third Millennium

Reflections by U.S. Bishops on the 30th Anniversary
of Decree on the Apostolate of the Laity from Vatican Council II

When was Vatican Council II?

Vatican II took place from October 1962 to December 1965. Four sessions of approximately two months each took place during that four-year period.

Who called it?

Blessed Pope John XXIII. Upon his death in June 1963, Pope Paul VI continued to convene the council.

Who attended?

2,860 bishops attended from all over the world, along with up to 80 observers from major Christian denominations.

What were the results?

- 4 constitutions (set direction for the whole church)
- 9 decrees (set a pace and direction for further discussion)
- 3 declarations (statements of theological position)
- 16 documents

Most profound impact of the 16 documents was in these four areas:

- *Church* renamed itself *The People of God*, all people are a vital living family instead of a building or an institution or just the hierarchy.
- *Liturgy* was renewed and became "the work of all the people." Its purpose was to energize and renew the Christian community.
- *Laity* was reminded of its primary call to holiness at baptism and its call to ministry as in the early church.
- *Ecumenism* = All persons are equal in God's family. All are encouraged to have a relationship of mutual *respect* and *dialogue* with non-Catholics and non-Christians.

Note to Staff Liaisons and Coordinators of MOMS:

Participants deserve to have their hands on the actual document and to read and reflect on what it means in their lives. In Session 8, the Facilitators need to facilitate and assist the Staff Liaison using adult spiritual formation techniques to call forth the gifts of the Spirit present in each person and encourage and invite them each to continue to share those gifts in the parish.

For more information, read or review:

Huebsch, Bill, with Paul Thurmes. *Vatican II in Plain English: The Constitutions*. Allen, Texas: Thomas More, 1996.

Resources for Christian Living. *The Faithful Revolutions: Vatican II in Plain English*. Allen, Texas: Resources for Christian Living. Set of videos $89.95. Tel.: 1-800-822-6701.

Called & Gifted for the Third Millennium:
Study Guide to Prepare for MOMS Session 8

We are all "the people of God" living in a new millennium. We each make a choice about how much we want to be a part of God's family. The church recognizes the talent and potential of the laity and encourages us to contribute to the building of God's family. We all, laity and clergy, need to have an open mind about new concepts, terminology, attitudes and practices. With the guidance of the Holy Spirit, people are feeling the call in four aspects of life: (1) holiness, (2) community, (3) ministry, and (4) Christian maturity.

This Study Guide, with space for your thoughts, is provided to assist you in making this document practical for your own life. You will be invited to share your thoughts during Session 8. Please jot down your answers to the questions after each section.

1. The Call to Holiness

Holiness requires effort and commitment to live the Beatitudes and to live an "ever more intimate union with Christ" (*Catechism of the Catholic Church*, 2014).

a. A common thread in the laity's account of their spiritual lives is the value of healthy relationships. The bonds of family and friendship, of neighborhood and parish are vital to lay women and men. These relationships help them form even deeper bonds of unity with Jesus Christ and a means of grace.

b. Three characteristics of the Call to Holiness:
- Suffering — Romans 5:34
- Service — Generosity of time and talent given to others
- Simplicity of lifestyle

How can you strengthen yourself for your Call to Holiness?

2. The Call to Community

"From the communion that Christians experience in Christ there immediately flows the communion which they experience with one another: All are branches of a single vine, namely, Christ" (*Christifideles Laici* 18). Each person has a great desire to belong to a group of people who share their same Christian values and faith. "Beyond the intimate community of family life, the parish is for most Catholics their foremost experience of Christian community, enabling them to express their faith" (pg. 10). Some groups grow into lifetime Christian friendships. A few examples of small communities are:
- Faith-Sharing Groups: Renew, MOMS.
- Support Groups: Bereavement, Alanon, AA
- Movements: Cursillo, Marriage Encounter
- Third Order: Benedictine Oblates, Dominican and Franciscan Lay Associates
- Adult Education: Scripture Study, History of Church

How do you experience the Call to Community?

3. The Call to Mission and Ministry

Every Christian is called to participate actively in the church's mission of bringing Christ's love to the human family with the reception of the sacraments.

a. Baptism, confirmation and Eucharist empower all believers to share in some form of ministry. The clergy and parish staff are challenged to call forth, identify, coordinate and affirm the many talents and gifts bestowed by the Spirit.

b. The laity share their faith through teaching children and youth and serving other adults in:
- peace and justice projects
- soup kitchens and shelters
- marriage preparation
- bereavement programs
- ministry to parents and families
- ministry to separated and divorced

All these actions, when performed in the name of Jesus, are forms of ministry that strengthen the Body of Christ and pass on the faith.

How do you share in the Call to Mission and Ministry?

4. The Call to Christian Maturity

The Gospel image of the vine and the branches reveals to us the image of a vital relationship with Christ, and it suggests the call to a continual process of maturation and growth.

a. Christian maturity requires that all of us, lay and ordained, provide the best teaching and example possible to our youth. The church pledges its support to parents and families as they seek to undertake their responsibilities as primary religious educators of their children. The purpose of MOMS is to strengthen the mother and, through her, the whole family in the practice of faith traditions and rituals.

b. A major challenge is to bring our Catholic tradition to life in the hearts, minds, and spirits of the next generation. All are called to the task of handing on the faith traditions to all God's children, for example, through Advent and Lenten Family Prayer and activities.

Name the faith traditions and rituals that you want to pass on to the next generation.

Please bring this Study Guide completed to Session 8.

Rules for Ongoing Groups

- **Punctuality:** Start and end on time. I will be punctual.

- **Anonymity:** I will not reveal what someone else has personally shared in the group with anyone outside the group.

- **Respect and Trust:** I will respect the right of each person to have her own thoughts, feelings, and beliefs based on her knowledge and life experience. I will trust that my dignity and life experience will be respected as well.

- **Non-Judgment:** I will not judge others. Feelings are not right or wrong. Each person has unique, valuable life experiences.

- **Gentleness:** I will be kind and gentle with myself and others. Hurting persons tend to reach out and hurt other persons. Healing persons tend to reach out with healing compassion.

- **Listening:** I will listen attentively and will not interrupt when another person is talking.

- **Sharing:** I will focus on my true self and try to use first person (I, me, myself) in my conversation. I give myself the freedom to share or pass. I will allow time for each person to share.

- **Rescuing:** I will not preach, editorialize, give advice, or try to problem-solve and/or rescue others. Each person has an ability to solve her own problems.

- **Cross-Talk and Interruptions:** I will not laugh at someone who is talking. I will not talk to others during another person's sharing. I will not interrupt.

- **Mutual Responsibility:** As the group continues to meet, I will take my turn as a facilitator. Leadership rotates among the members; this allows me to strengthen my facilitator/leadership skills at my own pace.

MOMS: Developing A Ministry

Sample Invitation to the Celebration of New Beginnings

To use the invitation on the following page "as is," white out the designated places and fill in with your own information. Make copies, then fold in half twice. For a nice effect, copy on a parchment-type paper.

You are invited to attend and express your support for MOMS in your community.

Date: *(Insert date here)*

Place: *(Insert location of celebration here)*

Time:
Appetizers and cocktails:	*(Insert time here)*
Opening Prayer:	*(Insert time here)*
Sit-down dinner:	*(Insert time here)*
Featured speaker:	*(Insert time here)*
Presentations:	*(Insert time here)*
Closing Prayer:	*(Insert time here)*

Cost: *(Insert cost here) per person.*

R.S.V.P. *Please extend to our organizing committee the courtesy of a reply as soon as possible.*
(Details for R.S.V.P. here)

Celebration of New Beginnings
in honor of
Ministry of Mothers Sharing

Sample Certificate

For a nice effect, copy the certificate on the following page on a parchment-type paper.

APPENDIX B:
Forms

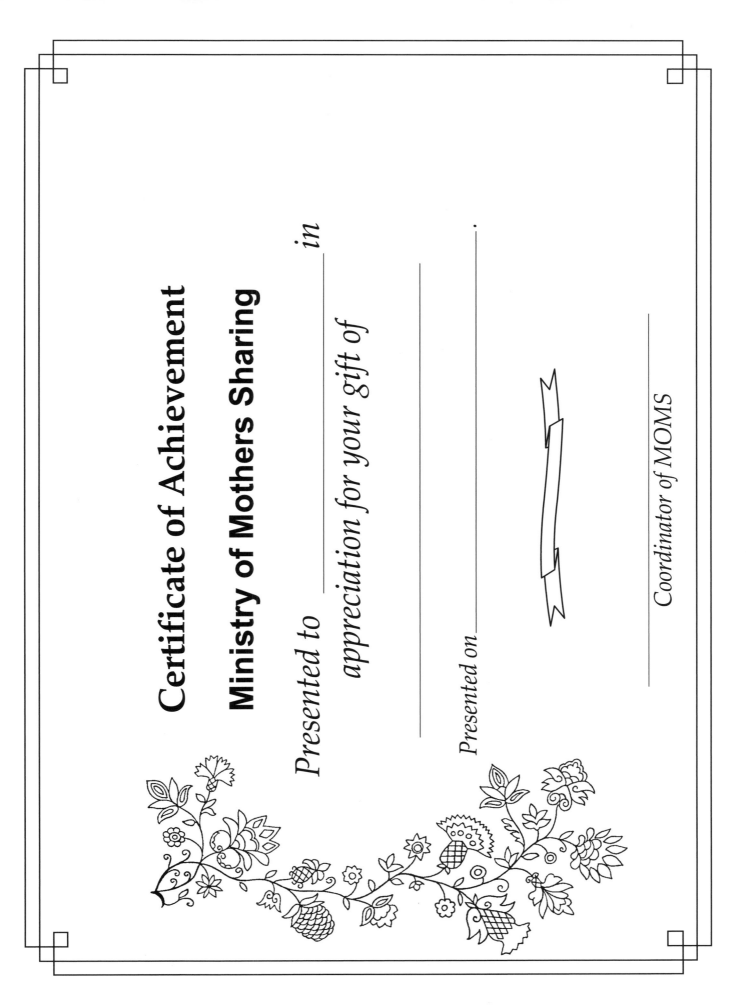

Certificate of Achievement

Ministry of Mothers Sharing

Presented to _____ *in*

appreciation for your gift of _____

_____ .

Presented on _____

_____

Coordinator of MOMS

Logo of Mary and Elizabeth

Use this logo in publicity brochures and other MOMS literature. Reduce in size and use on letterhead.

Mary shared her feelings with Elizabeth.

"How much it meant to share the faith, the fear, the anticipation with a trusted friend"...

THE VISITATION

Order the Complete MOMS Resources Here!

MOMS: Developing a Ministry 3rd Edition

Paula Hagen & Patricia Hoyt

Paper, $39.95, 200 pages,
8½" x 11",
ISBN 0-89390-534-8

This comprehensive manual is filled with resources and guidelines for setting up the Ministry of Mothers Sharing (MOMS) program within any church community. It includes detailed lesson plans, job descriptions for leaders, administrative and publicity procedures, and reproducible handouts that will make implementing your program a breeze.

MOMS: Facilitator's Guide 3rd Edition

Paula Hagen, Vickie LoPiccolo Jennett, & Patricia Hoyt

Paper, $23.95, 192 pages,
8½" x 11",
ISBN 0-89390-509-7

The *Facilitator's Guide* includes everything both the first-time and seasoned facilitator need to lead a MOMS group.

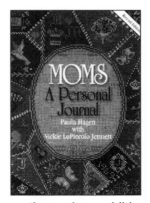

MOMS: A Personal Journal Revised Edition

Paula Hagen with Vickie LoPiccolo Jennett

Paper, $11.95, 112 pages,
7" x 10",
ISBN 0-89390-508-9

In this resource for mothers whose children are at home, readers are guided through a series of reflections that allow them to look at their values and the choices they make each day as well as to ponder the love they share with others in their lives. *A Personal Journal* examines the challenges of motherhood as they impact a woman's life: self-acceptance, stress, spirituality, feelings, personal growth and friendships.

A PRAYER COMPANION FOR MOMS

Vickie LoPiccolo Jennett with Paula Hagen

Paper, $7.95, 104 Pages,
4" x 6",
ISBN 0-89390-265-9

This purse-sized book is for all women who recognize a dimension of the spirituality found in the challenges and joys of motherhood. The authors offer reflections on such everyday experiences as juggling schedules, cleaning the refrigerator, waiting in line, and taking time out for fun. Keep a pen handy, too, because there's space for you to write your own thoughts and feelings too.

Order from your local bookseller, or use the order form on the last page.

More Community Ministry Resources

MINISTRY TO THE HOMEBOUND A 10-Session Training Course

Kent C. Miller

Paper, $29.95, 176 pages, 8½" x 11", ISBN 0-89390-268-3

Here is everything you need for a ten-session course on ministering to the homebound: background on building a caring ministry, session plans, and handouts you are allowed to photocopy.

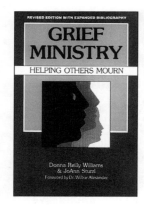

GRIEF MINISTRY Helping Others Mourn

Donna Reilly Williams & JoAnn Sturzl

Paper, $19.95, 232 pages, 5½" x 8½", ISBN 0-89390-233-0

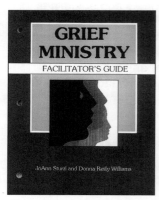

GRIEF MINISTRY Facilitator's Guide

JoAnn Sturzl & Donna Reilly Williams

Paper, $29.95, 120 perforated pages, 8½" x 11", ISBN 0-89390-227-6

Grief Ministry: Helping Others Mourn fills the need for an up-to-date resource that combines spiritual and psychological insights about griefwork. It covers general aspects of grieving, empathy, communication, listening, and prayer. The authors share insights on handling difficult situations, including such special cases as suicide, the death of a baby, job loss, AIDS, and divorce.

The *Facilitator's Guide* shows how to set up a program to train grief ministers using *Grief Ministry: Helping Others Mourn* as a textbook. The guide includes group listening and role-playing exercises, scenarios for discussion, a resource listing, and useful handouts with photocopy permission included.

Order from your local bookseller, or use the order form on the last page.

Small-Group Resources

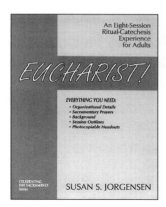

EUCHARIST
An Eight-Session Ritual-Catechesis Experience for Adults

Susan S. Jorgensen

Paper, $29.95, 208 pages, 8½" x 11", ISBN 0-89390-293-4

"Susan Jorgensen has created a living, breathing, working process for community transformation …. Respectful of differences, open to the variety of approaches, ready-to-use and well designed, it is a strong resource and strong spark to our ritual imaginations." — Catholic Press Association Book Award Judges

Participants in this eight-week program work through the prayers of the eucharistic liturgy, from opening rite to dismissal, and emerge with a deeper understanding of the words and gestures of the Eucharist.

WHY SMALL CHRISTIAN COMMUNITIES WORK

Msgr. Timothy O'Brien with Margaret Gunnell

Paper, 72 pages, $7.95, 5½" x 8½", ISBN 0-89390-371-X

The key to forming Christians is small Christian communities. In a small Christian community, says Msgr. Timothy O'Brien, you can't be anonymous. You have to share your faith — and relate to others as one of God's children. In so doing, you are embodying the human Jesus who saw himself as God's son and whose mission was to live out that belief. This little book is a must-read for all newly formed faith-sharing groups or anyone contemplating forming such a group.

LORD, YOU MUST BE JOKING!
Bible Stories That Tell *Your* Story

Eugene J. Webb

Paper, $10.95, 176 pages, 5½" x 8½", ISBN 0- 89390-309-4

Leader's Guide: Paper $7.95, 80 pages, 5½" x 8½", ISBN 0-89390-310-8

People remember stories. And that's what you get in this great resource from family therapist Eugene Webb. Great stories set into a biblical context with a twist that makes you think — about the story, about the Bible, about your story. Reflection questions help the process. A companion leader's guide helps you use the stories in retreats for adults or youth — or as a supplemental activity in family and other group situations.

STORIES TO INVITE FAITH-SHARING
Experiencing the Lord through the Seasons

Mary McEntee McGill

Paper, $8.95, 144 pages, 5½" x 8½", ISBN 0-89390-230-6

Sharing our stories makes our faith journey easier. These twenty stories are based on real life experiences that help us recognize God's presence in everyday life. Reflections and questions for group sharing can lead to personal awareness and prayer. Great for faith-sharing groups, workshops, and retreats.

Order from your local bookseller, or use the order form on the last page.

Small-Group Resources

MEN ARE NO DAMN GOOD (PENDING FURTHER RESEARCH)
Essays on Becoming a Man

Eugene J. Webb, Illustrated by C. P. Houston

Paper, $14.95, 192 pages, 5½" x 8½", ISBN 0-89390-343-4

Here's a book that unlocks one of the secrets of the universe: What is it with men anyway? But be warned, this is not a self-help book. "We men don't need help," says author Eugene Webb. "And you gals know by now that you're wasting your time slipping this or any book under our coffee cups or stuck behind our toothbrushes. We know what you're doing. It won't work." What guys need is to laugh at themselves, brag about themselves, and cry about themselves — and to have a good time doing it. So these witty essays about becoming a man are just a pleasure. Any helpful insights and unnerving pieces of wisdom are totally accidental.

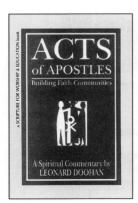

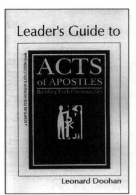

ACTS OF APOSTLES
Building Faith Communities

Leonard Doohan, PhD

Paper, $14.95, 240 pages, 5½" x 8½", ISBN 0-89390-292-6

Leader's Guide: Paper, $7.95, 48 pages, 5½" x 8½", ISBN 0-89390-300-0

Acts of Apostles breaks open major aspects of biblical teaching that you can put into practice immediately. Dr. Leonard Doohan's commentary will inspire you to adapt Luke's vision of church community as a blueprint for your own faith community-building. *Acts of Apostles* focuses on six topics: Luke, the author of Acts of Apostles; communities and community in Acts; Luke's purpose in writing Acts; images of God in Acts; life in the early church; and discipleship in Acts. In his final chapter, Dr. Doohan comments on each lectionary reading from Acts throughout the Easter season. The book includes indices of Scripture citations and topics and an extensive resource list. Great for parish study groups.

Order from your local bookseller, or use the order form on the last page.

A REMEMBERING HEART

Monica Brown

Songbook (Guitar, Lead Vocal): $9.95
Cassette: $9.98

This collection of contemporary music contains songs with spiritual mantras, which will make your prayer — personal or communal — more meaningful. The mantras will help you to remember, to ponder, and to come home to your center, where God makes sense. This album is an attempt by the artist to hold in sacred memory the moments and the times when she has known God in her life.

Contents: A Remembering Heart; In Memory Of You; So Much More; I Cry To You; We Sing Your Praise; Isn't It Beautiful; Song Of God's People; Holy Sacred Spirit; Gather Us O God; Speak Lord; Healing Is Your Touch; Shekinah / The Temple Of God; All Praise, Glory And Honour; My Soul Is Longing.

THE CHILD WITHIN
Music for Healing and Recovery

Julie Barrett Smith

Songbook (Keyboard, Guitar, Lead Vocal): $9.95
Cassette: $9.98

This powerful collection, born out of the composer's own season of grieving and healing, has many applications — from personal work to small-group work to liturgy. Ten evocative songs are contemporary and diverse in style, with lyrics that are touching and thought provoking. They are especially helpful for those who are on the journey of healing and memory.

Contents: The Child Within; Breaking The Silence; Little Orphan Annie; Broken People; One Day At A Time; Serenity; Humpty Dumpty — Like A Bone; If You Really Knew Me; That's All I've Wanted; This Too Shall Pass.

WRITING YOUR WAY TO WHOLENESS
Creative Exercises for Personal Growth

Terre Ouwehand

Paper, $17.95, 240 pages, 6" x 9", ISBN 0-89390-312-4

Are you trying to grow spiritually? If you are a budding writer — or you just enjoy journalizing or scribbling on napkins — here's good news. Terre Ouwehand, a creative writing instructor, uncovers the link between your most casual writing and your spiritual growth. Try her tips on freewriting, list-making, clustering, and streamwriting. Select from hundreds of exercises to uncover your creativity and discover your real feelings.

Order from your local bookseller, or use the order form on the last page.

Women's Resources

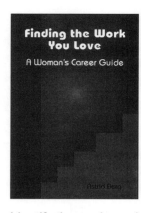

FINDING THE WORK YOU LOVE
A Woman's Career Guide

Astrid Berg

Paper, $15.95, 216 Pages,
6" x 9", ISBN 0-89390-269-1

This book is packed with information and exercises that will lead you to identify the work you love. Once you've focused your interests and used the author's tips for researching career and educational opportunities, read the final chapter on decision-making.

FINDING THE WORK YOU LOVE
Guided Visualizations

Astrid Berg

Audiocassette, 60 minutes, $11.95

This companion audiotape to *Finding the Work You Love: A Woman's Career Guide* will lead you through the visualization exercises found in the book. The tape can also be used by itself for group or individual exercises.

Order Form

Order these resources from your local bookstore, or mail this form to:

Resource Publications, Inc.
160 E. Virginia St. #290-OT
San Jose, CA 95112-5876
(408) 286-8505
(408) 287-8748 FAX

☐ My check or money order is enclosed.

☐ Charge my ☐ VISA   ☐ MC.

Expiration Date _____

Card # _____-_____-_____-_____

Signature _____

Name (print)_____

Institution_____

Street _____

City/State/Zip_____

QTY	TITLE	PRICE	TOTAL

Subtotal: _____

CA residents add 8% sales tax: _____

Postage and handling
($5 for order up to $50;
10% of order over $50 but less than $150;
$15 for order of $150 or more): _____

Total: _____